The Tree of Life for Youth

God's Promise of Salvation

Illustrated by
Anthony VanArsdale

CONCORDIA PUBLISHING HOUSE • SAINT LOUIS

Copyright © 2022 Concordia Publishing House
3558 S. Jefferson Avenue, St. Louis, MO 63118-3968
1-800-325-3040 • cph.org

Unless otherwise noted, Scripture quotations are from the
ESV® Bible (The Holy Bible, English Standard Version®),
copyright © 2001 by Crossway, a publishing ministry of Good
News Publishers. Used by permission. All rights reserved.

Manufactured in the United States of America

1 2 3 4 5 6 7 8 9 10   31 30 29 28 27 26 25 24 23 22

Table of Contents

The Beginning of Our Story

Creation

God has always been. He had no beginning and He will have no end. He always was, always is, and always will be—Father, Son, and Holy Spirit.

God chose to create the universe and with it, time began. The first verse of the Bible reads,

In the beginning, God created the heavens and the earth. (Genesis 1:1)

God created the heavens and the earth out of nothing at all, simply by the power of the words He spoke. Our earth was covered with water and there was no light at all, only thick darkness. And the Holy Spirit was hovering above those waters.

And God said, "Let there be light," and there was light. (Genesis 1:3)

God separated the light from the darkness, calling the light day and the darkness night.

On the second day, God stretched out the skies. On day three, God gathered the waters together and made the dry land appear. He spoke, and all kinds of plants covered the earth, including fruit trees.

On the fourth day, God spoke and created the sun, the moon, and all the stars and planets. They light up the earth during the day and shine on us during the night. They also help us keep track of the months, seasons, and years.

On day five, God filled the sky with animals that fly and the water with animals that swim.

On day six, God made all the animals that run, hop, slither, and crawl across the land. And last of all, on the same sixth day, He made humans. He made humans in His image. That means, they were able to know and love God. And just like God, they were good, loving, and kind. God's plan was for all of us people to love each other and watch over the animals on earth. We would care for all of them and make their world an ever better place to live.

God looked at everything He had made and He was very pleased. It was a very good world, the perfect place for humans, plants, and animals.

Name something bad in your life you wish you could change. *What do you think it would be like if our world and all of us people were still as good as when God first made us?*

God Creates the First Man and Woman

In the first chapter of Genesis, God gave us the big picture of how He created the heavens and the earth and everything in them. In chapter 2, He shows us how He made the first man and the first woman. First, He carefully formed the man's body from the ground. Second, He breathed the breath of life into his nostrils and the first man came to life.

But God saw it was not good for the man to be all alone in the world. So after bringing all the animals to Adam for him to name them, God caused Adam to fall into a deep sleep. And He took a rib from Adam's side and formed the body of the first woman with it. He brought her to Adam, who loved her and named her Eve. God joined them together as husband and wife. They would have children, and from those children God raised the whole human family that fills the earth today.

God planted a beautiful garden called the Garden of Eden and brought Adam and Eve to live in it. They were to watch it and take care of it. God met with them there and they were very happy. There, God planted two special trees. One was the tree of life, and if Adam and Eve would eat from it, they would live forever. The other was the tree of the knowledge of good and evil. God gave them one command in the garden—to not eat the fruit that grew on the tree of the knowledge of good and evil. He warned them that the day they ate from it, they would surely die.

Try to think of how God wants us to live with our family and friends. *What things can you do at school or home today to make life better for the people God put in your life?*

Adam and Eve Fall into Sin

God had a wonderful plan for our world. It would be filled with beautiful plants and animals and kept by perfect humans who would love God and one another and make life wonderful for all the animals. If only it could have stayed that way! Sadly, our first parents failed to keep God's command, and everything fell apart. Here is that sad, sad story:

One day, a serpent came up to Eve in the garden. Satan, a fallen angel, spoke to Eve through the serpent. Adam was there with her. The serpent asked her if God had told them they could not eat from any tree in the garden. Eve told him God let them eat from every tree but told them not to eat from the tree in the midst of the garden, or they would die.

That's when the serpent lied to her,

> **You will not surely die. For God knows that when you eat of it your eyes will be opened, and you will be like God, knowing good and evil. (Genesis 3:4–5)**

Eve believed the serpent's lie. She thought he was telling the truth. She was excited about eating that fruit and becoming like God. She reached out and grabbed it, taking a big bite. Then she handed it to Adam, and he ate.

Suddenly, their world changed. The first thing they noticed was that they were naked. When they were sinless and holy, it had never bothered them, but now, they felt exposed and embarrassed. They grabbed some leaves from the trees of the garden and tried to make clothes to cover themselves, but that didn't work very well. They could never cover their guilt and shame.

Then they heard the sound of the Lord walking toward them in the garden. They were terrified of what God would do; they were afraid they would die, so they tried to hide themselves.

God would have been right if He decided to put Adam and Eve to death at that moment, as He had warned. Then you and I would never have been born. But God loved them—and us—too much to do that. Instead, He turned to Satan, the fallen angel who had spoken through the serpent, and announced His plan to save Adam and Eve and all of us, their children.

> **I will put enmity between you and the woman, and between your offspring and her offspring; He shall bruise your head, and you shall bruise His heel. (Genesis 3:15)**

Jesus is that Offspring of the woman who died in Adam and Eve's place—in your place and mine. When He was nailed to the cross, the devil bruised Jesus' heel, but by that cross, Jesus crushed his head. Jesus' death would conquer the power of death for God's people.

The rest of the Old Testament shows the hurt, pain, suffering, and death that came into God's creation because of Adam and Eve's disobedience. But over and over, God repeats His promise to send Jesus and reveals more and more about how Jesus will save us.

How does Jesus' victory over sin and death change how you live every day? How does it change the way you treat other people?

Cain and Abel

After Adam and Eve disobeyed God and ate the fruit He had forbidden, God made clothes for them from the skins of animals and drove them out of the Garden of Eden. They had to work very hard to grow their own food by farming the land. Though they could no longer walk with God and talk with Him as before, God did not leave them. He helped Adam and Eve remember His promise to send the Savior.

Adam and Eve began having children. The first son mentioned in the Bible is named Cain and the second is Abel. Cain worked the ground growing crops while Abel was a shepherd who kept sheep. Adam and Eve taught them about God's promised Savior.

One day, when Cain and Abel had grown up, they brought offerings to sacrifice to the Lord. God was pleased with Abel's sacrifice because it came from faith—Abel believed God's promise and loved God for making that promise. But God was not pleased with Cain's sacrifice, probably because Cain didn't want to give an offering.

When Cain saw that God was pleased with his brother's sacrifice but not his, he became very angry. God warned Cain how dangerous this anger was:

> Sin is crouching at the door. Its desire is for you, but you must rule over it. (Genesis 4:7)

God meant that Cain's anger was strong, and if he wasn't careful, it would take control and he would do something horrible. He needed to admit his sacrifice had been wrong and trust God's promise to forgive and accept him.

But Cain did not listen to God. He asked Abel to come out into a field to talk to him, then he struck him and killed him. When God asked Cain where Abel was, Cain acted like he didn't know and was not responsible for keeping track of Abel. God told Cain He knew what Cain had done. But God put a mark on Cain to protect him from any of his brothers who would want to attack him for killing Abel. God wanted to forgive Cain, but Cain refused to repent and went off to live the rest of his life without God.

With Abel dead and Cain dead to God, the promise of the Savior passed on to their brother Seth.

Think of the last time you got really angry. *What did you want to do? How would it help to think that your anger was like a lion trying to take control of you and God is there to help you take control over it?*

Noah and the Ark

As more children and grandchildren were born after Cain and Abel, more and more of them followed Cain's path. They lived without God, doing whatever mean things they wanted to their brothers, sisters, and cousins. At the same time, the line of faithful believers from Seth shrunk smaller and smaller. It hurt God's heart to see the hate and cruelty, the pain, suffering, and death that filled His creation. He finally regretted ever creating humans. He decided to send a huge, worldwide flood to destroy all life from the surface of the earth.

But God had mercy on one of Seth's descendants named Noah. By God's grace, Noah still believed in God's promise of the Savior. So God taught him how to build a giant ship—an ark. On that ship, He would save a single family, Noah and his three sons and their wives, and two of each species of the land animals and birds. The rain fell for forty days and forty nights, and water came gushing from underground until the flood waters rose to cover every mountain on earth. The waters of the flood destroyed all other humans and animals.

It took 150 days before that water started receding back down into the earth. Noah was in the ark for over a year before the earth dried out and God told him to leave and bring out the animals he had saved. Then Noah's family and the animals on the ark started having children and began to fill the earth again. God made a promise never to send such a huge flood to destroy the world again. He set His rainbow in the sky as a reminder of that great promise.

Sadly, as Noah's grandchildren and great-grandchildren grew up, they wandered off from faith in God just as Cain had done. Once again, the number of believers who held on to God and His promises grew smaller and smaller. So once again, God stepped into human history to keep His promise of sending the Christ. He chose another husband and wife to raise up one more family—a nation of believers.

How can going to church, reading your Bible, and praying help keep you from wandering away from God like other people do?

God's Plan for Abraham

God Calls Abraham

God saved Noah and his family from the flood. But as the years went by, many of Noah's descendants forgot God's salvation and drifted away from Him. They rejected God and His promise of a Savior. But God did not give up on them. Once again, God chose a husband and wife to do His special work.

God told Abram to leave his home and travel with his wife, Sarai, to a different land. God didn't tell them where they were going, but He led them along the way. He promised to make a great nation of Abram's descendants, and one of them would be the Savior promised to Adam and Eve. God gave them new names, Abraham and Sarah, to mark His promises to them.

But there was one problem: Abraham was already seventy-five years old and Sarah was sixty-five, and they had not been able to have a child when they were younger. Now both of them were too old to have a baby. But God promised that by His mighty power, He would give them a baby. Though he waited a long time for a son and experienced challenges along the way, Abraham believed God's promise, and that faith in His promised Savior made Abraham and Sarah God's children.

How would you feel if you had to leave all of your friends and neighbors behind and move to a totally new place?

Abraham Offers Isaac

God led Abraham and Sarah to a land called Canaan. Abraham began building altars and telling the people of the land about God's promised Savior. God was already blessing the nations through Abraham.

But Abraham and Sarah spent many years in Canaan—twenty-four to be exact—and still had not had a baby. Then, one afternoon, when Abraham was ninety-nine and Sarah was eighty-nine, God appeared to Abraham with two angels. Abraham and Sarah thought they were three strangers passing by. They invited them to rest awhile and prepared a nice meal for them.

After the meal, the Lord promised Abraham that within a year, Sarah would give birth to the child God had promised. Sarah was listening inside her tent and laughed to herself when she heard the stranger, the Lord, make this promise. She didn't believe Him. But God kept His word. Abraham and Sarah's promised boy was born, and God told them to name him Isaac, which means "he laughs."

Some years later, God tested Abraham:

> Take your son, your only son Isaac, whom you love, and go to the land
> of Moriah, and offer him there as a burnt offering on one of the moun-
> tains of which I shall tell you. (Genesis 22:2).

They set out on their journey the next morning. When they reached that mountain, Isaac carried up the wood for the sacrifice. At the mountaintop, Abraham tied up Isaac and was just about to kill him when God, through His angel, stopped him and showed him a ram caught in a thorny thicket by its horns. God told Abraham to sacrifice the ram in place of Isaac.

God was giving Abraham and all his descendants a picture of the way Jesus would save us. Like Isaac, Jesus would carry the wood up the mountain—His cross. And like the ram, Jesus' head would be encircled with a crown of thorns and He would be sacrificed on the cross in the place of all sinners.

The picture of Jesus' great sacrifice that would save us was coming clearer. He would crush the serpent's head, meaning that He would remove the curse of sin from us by taking that curse upon Himself. Near this same mountain, about two thousand years later, God the Father would sacrifice His only begotten Son, crowned with thorns, to save us from our sins.

When in your life does God feel the furthest away and why? How can Christ's promise that He is with you always help you feel better in those times?

The Twins

When Isaac grew up, his mother, Sarah, died. Abraham sent his servant back to his relatives to bring a wife for Isaac. Her name was Rebekah. God gave Rebekah twin sons and told her they would grow into two great nations. He told her that the younger would be greater than the older.

Isaac and Rebekah named their twins Esau and Jacob. They were exact opposites. Esau loved the outdoors and was a hunter. Jacob was quieter, preferring to stay around the tents with his mother. Though Isaac knew God had chosen Jacob, Esau was his favorite.

Neither of the twins thought about God very much, nor His glorious promise of the Savior. Esau was born first, which meant he had the right to be in the line that would lead to the promised Savior. But one day, he was so hungry that he sold that right to Jacob for a bowl of stew.

Later, Rebekah learned Isaac was ready to give Esau the blessings of God after he came back from hunting and cooking a meal for him. Isaac was nearly blind, so she dressed Jacob in Esau's clothes, and Isaac gave Jacob the blessings he planned to give to Esau. When Esau found out, he wanted to murder Jacob. But Rebekah and Isaac sent Jacob to her brother Laban.

While Jacob was travelling there, he stopped one night to sleep. In a dream, he stood at the bottom of a staircase that reached up to heaven. He saw angels going up and down on the staircase and God standing at the top. God said to Jacob,

> Behold, I am with you and will keep you wherever you go, and will bring you back to this land. For I will not leave you until I have done what I have promised you. (Genesis 28:15)

Isn't it amazing that God kept giving His promises and blessings to a family that didn't always take Him seriously? God kept His promises to them and took care of them, just as He takes care of us and keeps all His promises to us, no matter how many times we don't take Him as seriously as we should.

Why do you think there are things that seem more important to us than God's promises in the Bible and our Savior, Jesus Christ?

12

Jacob's Wives and Twelve Sons

After his dream of God at the top of the staircase, Jacob traveled to his uncle Laban. Laban welcomed him, and Jacob became a shepherd of Laban's flocks. Because of the blessing Isaac had given him, the flocks under Jacob's care grew larger and larger, and Laban became a wealthy man. Jacob fell in love with Laban's daughter Rachel. When Laban found out, he offered to let Jacob marry her if he stayed and shepherded his flocks for seven years.

But at the end of those seven years, Laban was afraid Jacob would go away after he married Rachel. So on their wedding night, Laban tricked Jacob and gave him Leah, Rachel's older sister, instead. Because of the darkness, Jacob didn't recognize her. Of course, Jacob was angry the next day, but Laban promised if Jacob worked another seven years, he could marry Rachel also. So Jacob was married to two sisters, Leah and Rachel.

Jacob really loved Rachel, but Leah wanted Jacob to love her too. When God saw how miserable Leah was, He gave her four sons and a daughter. Leah's fourth son was Judah. He was the son God chose to continue the line that would lead to Jesus, the promised Savior.

God gave Leah more sons. Finally, after Jacob had ten sons, God answered Rachel's prayer and gave her a baby boy named Joseph.

In all, Jacob lived with Laban for twenty years. God gave him great herds and flocks even though Laban kept trying to cheat Jacob. Then God told Jacob it was time to return home. Jacob was afraid to meet his brother, Esau, because he thought he may still be mad enough to kill him. The night before they met, Jacob came across a stranger and started wrestling with him. He might have thought it was Esau, but it turned out to be God Himself. God changed Jacob's name:

> **Your name shall no longer be called Jacob, but Israel, for you have striven with God and with men, and have prevailed. (Genesis 32:28)**

Israel is the name of the nation that grew from Jacob's descendants.

When Jacob met Esau the next morning, Esau was very happy to see him. Even though Jacob had treated him so badly, God gave Esau the strength to forgive him. God forgave our entire sinful human family through His Son, Jesus, our Savior.

Describe a time you were scared about what someone else might do to you. *How did God help you at that time?*

Sold as a Slave

Jacob's favorite wife was Rachel, and her firstborn son, Joseph, was Jacob's favorite son. Jacob treated Joseph far better than all his other sons. Joseph made it worse when God gave him dreams of how great he would become, and he boasted about it to his brothers.

Everything exploded one day when Leah's sons were shepherding the flocks far away from home. The older brothers saw Joseph coming over the hills toward them, wearing an expensive robe their father had given him. They hated him so much that they made plans to kill him, but then they decided to sell him into slavery in Egypt instead. When they got home, they lied to their father and told him Joseph was killed by wild animals.

In Egypt, Joseph was sold to an Egyptian official, Potiphar. But even as a slave, God was with him. Joseph was loyal, worked hard, and was very honest. Potiphar saw how good Joseph was and put him in charge of everything in his house and business. But then Potiphar's wife lied about Joseph and falsely told her husband that Joseph tried to attack her. Potiphar was furious and put Joseph in prison.

Even in prison, God was with Joseph. The jailors started putting more and more prisoners in Joseph's care. More than two years later, Pharaoh, king of Egypt, had a dream that really scared him. He told his dream to his wise men, but no one could tell him what it meant. Then one of Pharaoh's servants remembered Joseph. He had been in prison with Joseph, and had a scary dream. Joseph had told him what the dream meant, and it came true.

So Pharaoh ordered Joseph to be brought to him. Pharaoh told Joseph he had two dreams. In the first, seven fat cows were grazing and suddenly seven thin, ugly cows came up and ate them—but they were still as thin and ugly as before. In the second dream, Pharaoh saw seven full, good ears of corn growing near the river. Then they were swallowed up by seven thin and ugly ears. Joseph told Pharaoh Egypt would have seven good years where the farms would grow a lot of food. Then Egypt would have seven bad years where nothing would grow, and Egypt would be very, very hungry.

Joseph advised Pharaoh to store up grain in the coming good years so he could feed the people during the famine. Pharaoh freed Joseph from prison and had him sit at his right hand. Joseph had the job of storing up the food and leading all of Egypt. Joseph was able to provide food not only for Egypt, but for many neighboring nations too. When Joseph's brothers ran out of food, they came to Egypt to buy some. Joseph tested them to see if they were truly sorry for selling him as a slave. Then, when he learned they were, he revealed himself to them. Joseph brought all of his father's family to live in Egypt where they grew into a great nation.

Joseph teaches us a lot about the life of Jesus, the promised Savior. Like Joseph, Jesus would be rejected by His own brothers and taken in chains to the ruler of another nation—the Roman governor. But through His suffering, Jesus would save all people from their sins, rise on the third day, and ascend to the Father's right hand in heaven. There, He governs all things that happen in creation for the good of His Church.

What is one way God has called you to help take care of your family or your friends? Pray that God would strengthen you to do that with joy and faith.

The Passover Lamb

God Calls Moses to Rescue Israel

Joseph's brothers and their families remained in Egypt for four hundred years and grew into a great nation, just as God had promised. But after many years, a new Pharaoh came to power who didn't know about Joseph and how he had saved Egypt. He treated the Israelites badly and made them slaves. God's people cried out to Him in their suffering. He heard them and raised up a deliverer named Moses.

When Moses was born, Pharaoh was so scared of how numerous the people of Israel were becoming that he commanded all of Israel's baby boys to be thrown into the Nile River. Moses' mother put him in a water-proof basket in the Nile River. Pharaoh's daughter found the basket, felt sorry for the baby inside, and adopted him as her own son. She named him Moses and raised him as a prince of Egypt in Pharaoh's own house.

But Moses knew he was an Israelite. When he was forty years old, he attacked and killed an Egyptian who was beating an Israelite slave. When Pharaoh found out, he was angry. Moses ran away from Egypt, crossed the wilderness, and lived in a country called Midian.

Moses married a Midianite woman, had two sons, and became a shepherd of his father-in-law's flocks. One day, forty years later, when he was eighty years old, he saw a bush burning on Mount Sinai. But the fire did not burn up the bush, so Moses went to check it out. God called to him from the burning bush:

> **Come, I will send you to Pharaoh that you may bring My people, the children of Israel, out of Egypt. (Exodus 3:10)**

Moses was afraid to go back to Egypt and face Pharaoh. But God gave him courage.

Describe something you had to do that seemed way too big and scary for you.

The Ten Plagues

Moses went back to Egypt to tell Pharaoh what God had commanded:
Let My people go. (Exodus 5:1)

Pharaoh was proud and stubborn; he refused to obey. So God sent a series of plagues, or disasters, to convince Pharaoh to change his mind. The plagues started out small: turning the Nile River into blood, filling Egypt with frogs, gnats, and flies. But Pharaoh kept refusing.

So God made the plagues stronger, and the Egyptians began to suffer more and more. The Egyptians' farm animals all died, painful sores broke out on their skin, hail and fire destroyed their crops, and locusts ate up what was left. Still, Pharaoh refused to listen. So God sent thick darkness over the land for three days and three nights.

Still, Pharaoh refused to obey God. So Moses warned Pharaoh that God would send the tenth and last plague. The angel of death would pass through Egypt and kill all the firstborn males—even Pharaoh's own son.

To protect His people from the angel of death, God commanded the Israelites to kill a lamb and spread its blood over the doorways of their houses. When the angel of death saw the blood, it passed over the house, saving the firstborn sons. The Israelites called this the Passover. When Pharaoh's son died, he finally set Israel free.

This Passover is the third really clear picture in the Bible of the sacrifice of the coming Savior. Jesus is the true Passover Lamb who poured out His blood on the cross and marked our hearts when He baptized us. His blood will save us from eternal punishment on Judgment Day.

How is the Passover similar to what God did for us in Jesus' suffering and death? How can that change how you look at your friends, family, and classmates?

Mount Sinai

After Israel left Egypt, God led the Israelites to the shore of the Red Sea. Pharaoh changed his mind about freeing the Israelites and led his army to recapture them. When they came close to the Red Sea, God divided the waters so Israel could pass through the sea on dry ground. The Egyptians rode into the sea to catch them. But after the last Israelites reached the other side, God brought the waters back together and all the Egyptians drowned. The Israelites knew God had set them free, and they rejoiced.

God led them through the wilderness to Mount Sinai, the same place where He had appeared to Moses in the burning bush. This time, the whole mountain was burning with God's presence. In a booming voice, God spoke the words of the Ten Commandments to all the people so they would know, love, and trust in Him.

The Israelites were terrified by God's thundering voice, so they begged Moses to go up the mountain to listen to God. They promised they would do everything Moses told them. Moses spent forty days on the mountain with God. God gave him the Ten Commandments and the design for the tent of meeting, also called the tabernacle, a place where they would worship and God would meet with them. Here, they would burn sacrifices, and the Levites would carry the tabernacle from place to place across the wilderness.

After the tabernacle was built, Moses led Israel from Mount Sinai to the border of the Promised Land. Israel sent twelve spies to go through the land of Canaan. Ten of the spies brought a bad report, scaring the people as they talked about the mighty Canaanites. They made the people so scared that they didn't trust God and refused to go to war. So God made them turn around and wander through the wilderness for forty years until all the grown-ups who had refused to trust Him died. Israel's forty years of wandering are described in the Book of Numbers.

Shortly before he died, Moses preached a series of farewell sermons, which make up the Book of Deuteronomy. In those sermons, he made this promise, "The LORD your God will raise up for you a prophet like me from among you, from your brothers—it is to Him you shall listen" (Deuteronomy 18:15). Jesus Christ is that prophet. God's mighty Son came as our human brother to teach us about God and His love.

> Think of the rules your parents, or those who care for you, have for you. *How are they trying to protect you with these rules?* If you aren't sure, ask them. But be sure to ask them nicely!

17

Entering the Promised Land

After Moses died, God raised Joshua to lead Israel into the Promised Land.

Moses My servant is dead. Now therefore arise, go over this Jordan, you and all this people, into the land that I am giving to them, to the people of Israel. (Joshua 1:2)

Joshua led the Israelites up to the Jordan River, and God caused the river to stop flowing so the Israelites could cross through it on dry ground. That terrified the people of Canaan, especially the people who lived nearby in the town of Jericho, with its thick, tall wall.

God told Joshua to have the army of Israel and the priests carrying the ark of the covenant walk around the city one time for six consecutive days. Then, on the seventh day, they walked around the city seven times. Then each Israelite turned toward the city and shouted. God made the walls of Jericho crumble and fall, and the Israelites went in and captured the city.

God helped Joshua defeat the Canaanite nations and gave the land to Abraham's descendants as He had promised. By the time Joshua's work was done, the strength of the nations of Canaan was broken and the twelve tribes of Israel held the center of the Promised Land. God promised the twelve Israelite tribes He would make them grow strong enough to drive out the rest of the Canaanites and give them all the land God had promised to Abraham, Isaac, and Jacob.

God wanted Israel to serve Him the way He had taught them on Mount Sinai through Moses. He would forgive their sins and teach them to share His wonderful promise of a Savior with the nations around them. But the Israelites failed to obey God. They served the gods of the Canaanites and the other surrounding nations.

In order to turn His people back to Him, God brought in neighboring nations that conquered Israel and made their lives miserable. Just as in Egypt, the Israelites called out to God, and God raised up leaders called judges to deliver and govern them.

What is something God commands us not to do that seems like it would be so fun to do? How can remembering Jesus on the cross teach us not to do those things?

The Judges

The Book of Judges is a very sad book to read. The people of Israel kept turning their backs on God, doing whatever they thought would make them feel good.

Everyone did what was right in his own eyes. (Judges 21:25)

The problem with doing what is right in our own eyes, or satisfying our sinful desires, is those desires come from our sinful nature. Those sins seem really exciting at first but turn into traps that hurt God and other people. They fill us with guilt and hurt our reputation.

As God's people turned away from Him, He sent in enemy nations to show them what life would be like if He wasn't there to help and protect them. When they suffered, they remembered God and cried out for Him to save them from their enemies. God raised up leaders called judges, who drove out their enemies and led the people back to God.

But then when the judge died, the people forgot and turned away from God again. Over and over they suffered at the hand of other nations, got delivered by a new judge, then turned away again after that judge died.

God raised one final judge for His people—Samuel. Samuel was unique among the judges. He was not only a ruler but he was also a great prophet and a priest. He gave Israel a peek at the coming Savior, who would serve as King over all God's people. He is the great Prophet who teaches us about God's love and the great High Priest who offered Himself on the cross to take away our sins and win our forgiveness.

When Samuel grew old, the leaders of the people demanded, "Appoint for us a king to judge us like all the nations" (1 Samuel 8:5).

Sadly, they didn't understand their problem was their sin. They thought they just needed a strong king like every other nation, and that king would stop those bad things. In response, God told Samuel to anoint a humble, yet very tall and impressive young man as king. He was from the smallest tribe of Benjamin. The man's name was Saul.

Samuel anointed, or set aside, Saul as king and God filled him with the Holy Spirit. The Spirit gave Saul everything he would need to be a good king for Israel.

At first, Saul did well, delivering Israel from its enemies. But as he grew older, he became proud of the things he accomplished and forgot God made them possible. Instead of carefully following God's commands, he started doing what was right in his eyes. Does that sound familiar?

In time, God rejected Saul because of his disobedience and removed the Holy Spirit from him. Without the Spirit, Saul lost his courage and his confidence. He became fearful, suspicious, and insecure in his rule. God chose a new man, one who thought like God did. He would replace Saul as king of Israel.

Even though Israel rejected Him, God remained faithful to His promise to His people, just as He always remains faithful to His promises to you and me.

> Think of a time when you thought you knew better than God or what God's Word says, and it turned out really bad. Thank God that He remained faithful to you through Jesus, even though you failed.

19

Slaying the Giant

Saul Rejected, David Anointed

King Saul started out pretty good. After Samuel anointed him, the Holy Spirit filled him and gave him great courage to lead Israel. When he obeyed the Holy Spirit, everything went well.

But as Saul got older, he wasn't careful to follow God's instructions. He started doing the things he wanted and not doing the things he didn't want to do. He became proud of himself

and worried more about what his people thought of him than what God thought of him. Finally, the Lord rejected him as king of Israel and took His Holy Spirit away from him, and Saul lost his courage.

While Saul was still king, God secretly sent Samuel to the city of Bethlehem to anoint David king over Israel. When he was anointed, the Holy Spirit rushed upon David. The Holy Spirit gave him courage to fight and kill Goliath the giant when Saul and all the other Israelites were quaking in fear.

David served King Saul and was extremely loyal to him. David's courage and strength in the Spirit helped him lead Israel's army to great victories. Those great victories should have made Saul thankful—instead, they made him jealous. That jealousy filled him with suspicion that David would try to kill him to become king.

Several times, Saul tried to kill David. So David went into hiding while Saul hunted him with Israel's army. Twice, David had the chance to kill Saul, but he refused to hurt the king. Instead, he trusted God's protection and let God deal with Saul. Eventually, Saul was wounded in battle and killed himself because he feared what his enemies would do to him if they captured him.

David became king and defeated all of Israel's enemies. He won peace on every side and stretched Israel's boundaries to hold all the land God had promised to Israel. He captured Jerusalem and made it his capital. David brought the ark of the covenant into the city.

David wanted to build a magnificent temple in Jerusalem, but God would not permit him because of all the war and killing David had done to protect God's people. God wants to be known as a God of love, peace, and forgiveness, not a God of war, punishment, and death. God told David His temple would be built in a reign of peace—the reign of David's son Solomon. But God promised David He would build a house for him, that is, one of David's descendants would be the promised Savior, who would reign eternally. That is why Jesus is often called the Son of David in the Gospels.

Why is the relationship of a king to his subjects different than other leaders to the people under their authority? Why, do you think, is it so important for us to think of Jesus as our King?

Solomon's Rise and Fall

David was not a perfect king, but he mostly served God and loved and protected God's people, Israel. His young son Solomon became king after him. Solomon was making a great sacrifice to the Lord at the tabernacle at Gibeon when God appeared to him in a dream and told him to ask for whatever he wanted. Instead of asking for wealth or power, Solomon asked for wisdom to know how to lead God's great people. This pleased God greatly because Solomon wanted this wisdom to serve, lead, and protect God's people—the way his father, David, had ruled Israel.

God also gave Solomon great wealth and made him famous throughout the land. Solomon built the temple David had prepared. He built it on Mount Moriah, the same place God had provided a sacrifice for Abraham's son Isaac. Across from this very spot, Jesus, the final sacrifice, would one day suffer the wrath of God on a cross to bring forgiveness and eternal life to God's people.

Like Saul, Solomon started as a good and wise king, but when he got older, he broke several of God's laws. In particular, he broke God's command to Israel's kings not to marry women from other nations. Solomon married many foreign women and loved them, and they led him to idolatry. He built temples to his wives' false gods and even worshipped them. In response, God told Solomon He would take the kingdom from Solomon's son, but for David's sake, and God's promise of the Savior King, He would permit Solomon's descendants to reign over the tribe of Judah as king. Ten of the other tribes would be ruled by another Israelite king. After Solomon died, ten tribes north of Judah broke off and formed their own kingdom called Israel. David's descendants ruled the southern kingdom called Judah, which included the tribes of Judah and Benjamin. Solomon's idolatry resulted in the twin countries of God's people living in deep mistrust of each other.

What are some things your friends or kids at school like to do that could be harmful to your faith as a child of God? How can you still be friends without letting those things turn you away from God?

The Northern Kingdom, Israel

When Solomon's son, Rehoboam, refused to cut back the high taxes his father Solomon had charged, Israel was very unhappy. Ten tribes north of Judah broke away and formed their own kingdom called Israel. Their first king, Jeroboam, was afraid his subjects would return to the king of Judah when they went back to the temple for the Passover and other required feasts. So he built two temples of his own in the north and south ends of his kingdom. This false religion lasted through the whole history of the kingdom of Israel. Sadly, none of the kings of Israel after him ever returned to the Lord.

Israel in the north was ruled by a series of dynasties—fathers, sons, grandsons, and great-grandsons who ruled as king. All the kings of all these dynasties were wicked, some worse than others. Israel was larger and stronger than Judah, but the Israelite were very disobedient to the Lord. The wickedness was at its worst under King Ahab and his wicked queen Jezebel. So what did God do? He sent two of the greatest early prophets: Elijah and Elisha.

The first, Elijah, called Israel to repent and return to the Lord. When Ahab refused, God, through Elijah, declared a drought that lasted three and a half years. After this time, Elijah held a famous contest against the prophets of the false god Baal. Baal's prophets prepared an offering and kept calling on Baal for six hours to light it on fire—but nothing happened. Then Elijah prepared an offering for the Lord. Then he drenched it in water three times to make the wood really hard to light. Then he prayed to God and immediately fire came down from heaven and consumed the sacrifice, the wood, the water, and even the dirt and rocks. God made it clear—He was the only real God in all of Israel.

Elisha became an assistant to Elijah and continued as prophet after Elijah was taken up alive into heaven. By God's power, both Elijah and Elisha raised dead children. Elisha also cleansed a leper and performed other miracles by God's power. But despite these great prophets, the kings and people of Israel continued worshiping Baal and other false gods. Ultimately, God brought in the mighty Assyrian army to capture and exile the nation. The northern kingdom of Israel disappeared and are forever known as the Ten Lost Tribes.

Who do you know who knows the rules at home or school but keeps breaking them anyway? Why is it important for us to do what God wants and obey our parents and teachers?

The Fall of Judah

When God divided Israel into two kingdoms, David's descendants continued to rule in the south. This kingdom was made up of two tribes—Judah and Benjamin. The kings of Judah were a mix of good and evil kings. But among the faithful kings, two were especially like David with their hearts really devoted to the Lord: Hezekiah and Josiah.

Hezekiah was king in Judah at the time when God brought the Assyrian army to crush the northern kingdom of Israel. The Assyrians had the greatest army in the world at that time and swept south into Judah. They captured every walled city of Judah and finally surrounded Jerusalem. Helpless to drive away the Assyrians, King Hezekiah and the prophet Isaiah prayed to God. That same night, God sent an angel who killed 185,000 Assyrian soldiers. The Assyrians withdrew in panic and God saved the kingdom of Judah.

Josiah was the father of the last kings in Judah. He was eight years old when he became king, and he served the Lord all his days. When he was eighteen, he had the priests and Levites restore the temple, which had been neglected for generations. The workers rediscovered an important scroll of Scripture that had been lost. The scroll warned of what God would do if Israel turned away from Him and worshiped foreign gods. Josiah called the people of Judah to repent. Then he tore down the idols and high places in Judah. He even went into the land of Israel in the north and tore down the two temples Israel's first king, Jeroboam, had built. When Josiah died, his sons became king, one after the other. They turned Judah away from God again.

Judah lasted longer than Israel, but because its wickedness and idolatry grew worse and worse, God brought in Babylon, the empire that had conquered the Assyrians, to destroy Jerusalem and the temple and take the people of Judah off to exile. Now, just like the northern kingdom, Judah was conquered and scattered. It was in danger of disappearing just like Israel's ten tribes. But God kept His promises to His people, even in these darkest times.

Describe the darkest time in your life when you felt things would never get better. *What did God do for you?*

Judah in Exile

Judah was unfaithful to God. He brought in the Babylonians to destroy Jerusalem and the temple and take the people into exile, far from their homes. God had every right to punish Judah and never bring them back home. But He had made a promise to Adam and Eve to send a Savior. He had promised Abraham, Isaac, and Jacob that one of their descendants would be that promised Savior. And He had promised King David that one of his descendants would be the Messiah who would reign over Israel forever.

So during the roughly seventy years Judah was exiled in Babylon, God raised up great prophets and leaders to protect His people, remind them of His promises, and finally bring them back to Judah and Jerusalem when His time had come.

Jeremiah was a great prophet God raised up for Judah in the years before the fall, during the time of faithful king Josiah. After Babylon conquered Jerusalem, Jeremiah received permission to remain behind with the poor the Babylonians had left behind in Jerusalem and Judah. Jeremiah told them to repent and restore correct worship. Unfortunately, the people grew even more wicked and proud—thinking they were better than the Jews who had been sent into exile.

God didn't forget the exiles who had been taken off to Babylon. He raised up an exiled priest named Ezekiel. At first, the exiles were confident their time in Babylon would be short. Ezekiel told them their stay would be long. Then, when the exiles grew discouraged and convinced they would never return home, Ezekiel promised them God would bring them home and bring them the promised Savior.

One other problem threatened the exiles. The Babylonian king, Nebuchadnezzar, did not know or respect the Lord God. He thought his gods were stronger and that is why his army had defeated Israel. So God raised up a young man named Daniel and prepared him to serve in government in Babylon. He would teach the king about God and help protect the people of Judah until it was time to return to Jerusalem. There, they would rebuild the temple in preparation for the coming of the Christ. Even in such a dark time, God remained with His people.

Who has God put in your life to take care of you and help you grow into a man or a woman?

Delivered from the Lions

The Close of the Old Testament

Last week, we read about how God brought the Babylonians to destroy Jerusalem and the temple and drag the people of Judah into exile. Judah could have disappeared in Babylon, but instead, God raised up prophets like Jeremiah and Ezekiel and leaders like Daniel to preserve it through roughly seventy years of exile.

Daniel became a powerful prophet and successful government official in Babylon. When Babylon was defeated by the Persians, Daniel's life could have been in jeopardy as an official in the enemy government, but God protected him. Daniel found favor in the eyes of the Persian king, and he was promoted to a high position in the Persian empire. This caused intense jealousy in Daniel's enemies that led him to the lion's den.

When God saved Daniel, the Persian king raised him to his right hand and God worked through Daniel to protect the exiled Jews. Probably later that same year, the Persian king passed a new law permitting the Jews to return to Jerusalem and rebuild the temple. The exiled Jews rebuilt the temple despite great opposition from their neighbors, chiefly the Samaritans.

A few decades later, God raised up a Jewish orphan named Esther who was chosen to be the queen of the Persian emperor. She helped save the Jews from another disaster when a high-ranking government official tricked the king into ordering the destruction of all the Jews. She exposed his plot and the king gave the Jews permission to defend themselves and kill their enemies.

With many of the exiles back in Jerusalem and Judah, the temple rebuilt, and worship restored, it was nearly time for the Messiah to be born. Jesus would not be born for four hundred more years, but God's plan to send the Savior was on track.

Consider a position or role you have at home, at school, or on a team. *What opportunities has God given you to love and serve your neighbor?*

The Time Between the Old and New Testaments

The Old Testament came to a close less than a hundred years after the rebuilding of the temple. In the final book of the Old Testament, the prophet Malachi announced the coming Savior who would suddenly come to this new temple, and the prophet like Elijah who would precede Him. The Savior is Jesus and the prophet is John the Baptist.

Four hundred years passed between the close of the Old Testament and the birth of Christ. But huge changes took place during those years. The Persian Empire was destroyed by Alexander the Great from Macedonia. The Macedonian empires that followed Alexander were conquered by the Romans, who controlled the land of Israel when Jesus was born.

Shortly before Jesus was born, there was a civil war in Rome between two leaders who wanted to be the second emperor of Rome. A young ruler of Jerusalem named Herod helped the Roman Octavius become Emperor Caesar Augustus. Augustus named him King Herod and gave him a large territory to rule, including Jerusalem and the whole land of Israel. Now the world was set for the coming of the promised Christ.

Who are the people who govern your city, state, and country? Why should we pray for them?

Jesus' Birth

Finally, the time came for God to keep the great promise that He made to Adam and Eve in the Garden of Eden. God the Father chose a virgin named Mary, a descendant of David, from the northern town of Nazareth, to be the human mother of His Son. Jesus was conceived in Mary by the Holy Spirit's power.

Through the prophet Micah, God had told His people that the Christ would come not only from David's line but also from his hometown of Bethlehem. To move Mary from Nazareth to Bethlehem, God worked through the Roman emperor, Caesar Augustus. Augustus passed a law that required a census (or counting) of the entire Roman world. That meant Joseph, Jesus' human father, and all the Jews had to return to the hometown of their ancestors.

So Joseph took Mary to Bethlehem, David's hometown. While they were there, Mary gave birth to Jesus, the Savior God had promised throughout the Old Testament. Jesus entered our human history. He was born and raised through childhood like each of us. He learned what we learn and experienced the things we experience, yet He never once sinned. In Jesus, we have a God who understands what it is to live in this sinful world. He cares deeply for us and all those who feel hopeless and lost. He calls us to be His own brothers and sisters. Through Baptism and the Word of God, His Holy Spirit creates faith in Him so we never need to fear Satan or death because we are His forever.

What does it mean to live each day as God's redeemed child in Christ while also living your life with other people that God loves?

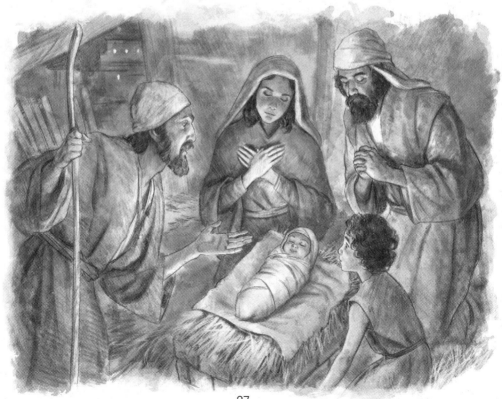

Jesus' Childhood

When Jesus was born, God placed a star in the sky, which was seen by the Wise Men or Magi, well-educated scholars and advisers to kings from countries east of Judea (Daniel and his three friends were trained as magi). They followed this star westward until they reached Jerusalem, where King Herod was ruling. When they asked where the King of the Jews was and explained how they followed His star, King Herod was stirred up with jealousy at a rival, upstart king. The Jewish priests told Herod Micah had prophesied that the Christ would be born in Bethlehem. So Herod told the Wise Men to go and worship Him, then return and send him word where the Child was so he could also go and worship Him—intending to kill this young rival instead.

The Wise Men traveled to where Jesus was, now a young boy with his parents. After the Wise Men found the house, they worshiped Jesus and gave Him their gifts. Then, being warned in a dream, they returned to their home without visiting Herod. When Herod learned he had been outsmarted, he ordered his soldiers to kill all the boys two years old and younger in Bethlehem, thinking he would do away with this rival king. But when the Wise Men left, an angel warned Joseph in a dream to flee to Egypt, so he left in the night with Mary and Jesus and escaped Herod.

After Herod died, Joseph planned to return to Judea. But after learning which of Herod's son was ruling in his place, he was scared to return to Bethlehem. Being warned in another dream, he took Mary and Jesus to her hometown of Nazareth where Jesus was raised. That is why He was known as Jesus of Nazareth and not Jesus of Bethlehem.

After that, we hear only one event from Jesus' childhood—when He was twelve years old. Every year, Joseph took his family to Jerusalem to celebrate the Passover. After the festival, Jesus' family began their trip home while He remained in the temple courts listening to the Jewish teachers and asking them questions. Mary and Joseph searched for Him frantically for three days. Finally, they found Him in the temple courts. When they asked Him why He had worried them so, Jesus answered, "Did you not know that I must be in My Father's house?" Luke 2:49). After this, Jesus went with them and was obedient to them. In the following years, He worked hard with Joseph, learning to be a carpenter. He developed His skills and a good reputation.

What difference does it make to know that Jesus experienced the same kind of childhood you are experiencing?

John the Baptist

Malachi, the final prophet of the Old Testament who had prophesied of Jesus' coming, had also foretold a forerunner who would be like Elijah, the great prophet. For this role, God raised up John the son of a priest, Zechariah, and his wife, Elizabeth, who was a cousin of Mary. Zechariah and Elizabeth were both old, like Abraham and Sarah. Like Sarah, Elizabeth was unable to have children and was past the age of childbirth. An angel appeared to Zechariah, just like God had appeared to Abraham and Sarah. The angel told him that they would have a son, but just like with Abraham and Sarah, Zechariah doubted. In spite of his doubt, by God's power, Elizabeth conceived. When he was born, they named him John, which means "the Lord has shown favor."

When he was grown, the Holy Spirit led John into the wilderness where he began preaching a Baptism of repentance, or turning away from sin for the forgiveness of sins. John's job was to break through the self-confidence of the Jewish people, to show they were all sinners who needed to repent and have their sins washed away by the coming Savior. He was preparing the people so Jesus could come and share the great love and grace of God, who had not forsaken His sinful people. Jesus would take their sin and guilt upon Himself and bring them into His gracious kingdom.

John confronted the hypocrisy of the leaders and baptized those who repented, teaching them true and faithful worship of God. John warned the people that the Messiah was living among them and would come to John to be revealed to Israel. Finally, one day, Jesus from Nazareth stood among the crowds of people coming to see John. What happened next set the stage for Jesus' mission and ministry for years to come.

> Think of a time when God's Word called you to repent and change one of your habits or an attitude. *What impact did that have on your life as God's redeemed child in Christ?*

Jesus Is Baptized into God's Plan

Jesus' Temptation

When Jesus was baptized by John in the Jordan, He was connected with all of us sinners who are baptized. He connected us to His life, death, and resurrection. As John pointed out, Jesus connected Himself to our sins:

> **The next day he saw Jesus coming toward him, and said, "Behold, the Lamb of God, who takes away the sin of the world!" (John 1:29).**

The first step in Jesus' journey to save us may seem kind of strange. The Holy Spirit led Him into the wilderness where He went without food for forty days and nights. All that time, He was being tempted by Satan. It may seem unusual, but that was the same way our human history started. After God made Adam and Eve, Satan came to the Garden of Eden and tempted them to disobey God and eat the forbidden fruit.

Where Adam and Eve were well fed, Jesus was extremely hungry. Where they were in a lush garden surrounded by fruit trees, He was in a barren wilderness surrounded by rocks. But Jesus stood firm, trusting His heavenly Father perfectly, where Adam and Eve quickly doubted God and gave in to temptation. Satan tempted Jesus to jump off the highest point of the temple to prove He trusted that God would send His angels to catch Him and keep Him safe. But Jesus knew He didn't have to prove His trust to Satan, and He refused. Finally, Satan tempted Jesus to bow down to him and cooperate with him so He wouldn't have to go to the cross. But once again, Jesus stood firm in God's Word and commanded Satan to leave Him. Then God the Father sent angels to take care of Jesus' hunger and all the needs of His human body.

Jesus overcame all of Satan's temptations for us and gives us His perfect life in exchange for our sinful lives. Then He continued to carry our sins toward the cross.

What does Jesus' experience of being tempted in the wilderness teach you about facing temptations to sin?

Jesus Calls Twelve Disciples

After His temptation, Jesus returned where He had been baptized and began gathering several disciples, or students who would follow Him. Taking those first disciples with Him, He returned to the northern part of Israel known as Galilee. There, He began to teach in the synagogues, or places of Jewish worship. He also taught in the towns and gathered other disciples until He had called a group of twelve specially chosen disciples. The Twelve would be the eyewitnesses He would use to build His Church after He had completed His earthly mission to save the world. They followed Him throughout His ministry as eyewitnesses, and their experiences and interactions with Jesus are recorded in the four Gospels.

There was really nothing special about these twelve men. Most of them were fishermen, several were brothers, one was a hated tax collector, and another a rebel who wanted to free Israel from Rome's power. In their lives and callings, we can see a glimpse of our lives as God's Church today. Christ has called us to saving faith and a life of following Jesus. Like them, we listen to Jesus' Word and share the Gospel so that more may hear and be called to saving faith.

Consider the main roles you have at home and at school. *What opportunities do those roles give you to tell others what Jesus has done for you through your words and actions?*

Jesus' Healing Miracles

Many Old Testament prophets had worked miracles by the power of the Holy Spirit, especially Moses, Elijah, and Elisha. To establish Himself as the promised Savior, Jesus worked an overwhelming number of miracles, especially healing miracles. It didn't matter if the person was blind, deaf, or unable to walk, Jesus was able to heal any and all who came to Him. This demonstration of His divine power showed that He was not just another prophet, but the promised Messiah, the Son of God.

But Jesus' true mission was not to simply be a physician or drive out demons. He came especially to teach us about God's kingdom and to go to the cross to heal our bodies and spirits for all time. The Old Testament prophet Isaiah described this as Jesus taking our illnesses upon Himself. He carried those sins from His Baptism to the cross where He would suffer their punishment and destroy them forever.

At the same time, Jesus' healing miracles give us a wonderful glimpse into what He will do on Judgment Day when He comes to restore all of God's creation. He will raise and glorify our bodies, making them perfect and immortal forever. It is so easy to think the end goal of our faith is spending eternity in the spiritual life in heaven. We will enjoy this after our bodies die, but Jesus' healings remind us Jesus will reunite our spirits with our glorious risen bodies. There, we will live with Him in the new heavens and the new earth forever.

How would your life be different today if you and your family did not have to worry about sickness, injury, or death?

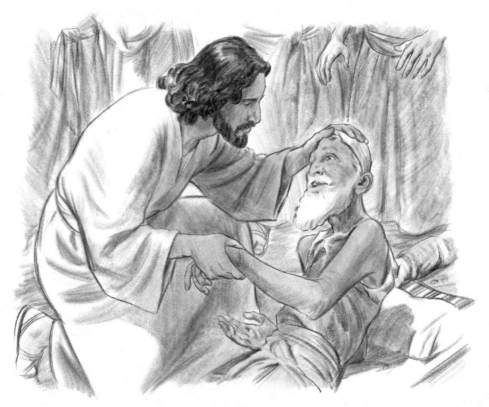

Jesus Raises the Dead

During His ministry, Jesus showed His concern and compassion for large crowds as well as individuals. Once, He spent all afternoon teaching a crowd. His disciples told Him it was getting late and He should send the crowd away so they could find food. But Jesus told them to feed the crowd. The Twelve said this was impossible, but Jesus had the crowd sit down. He took five loaves of bread and two fish, blessed the food, and divided it among the disciples. They handed the food to the crowd. It miraculously multiplied, satisfying the hunger of five thousand men besides the women and children with them.

In addition, as Jesus' ministry progressed, He continued His battle against Satan and his fallen angels. He drove demons out of people who were possessed by them. He simply commanded them and they were forced to obey. Jesus demonstrated His supreme, divine authority over the visible and invisible, the natural and supernatural.

Jesus even demonstrated His power over death by raising people who had died. The four Gospels give us three accounts of dead people whom He raised to life—the twelve-year-old daughter of a synagogue ruler named Jairus, the only son of a widow from the town of Nain, and Lazarus, the brother of Jesus' dear friends Martha and Mary. Again, Jesus gave us a glimpse of the Last Day, when He will raise all the dead, both believers and unbelievers, and judge all mankind. Though the victory for His people began and was assured at the cross, Jesus will crush the power of sin, death, and the devil once and for all at the final resurrection and restore His creation.

What is one blessing God has given you in your life that you easily overlook?

Jesus' Miracles in Creation

Jesus also showed His power over His creation several times. Most of these instances centered around the Sea of Galilee, the home base of Jesus and His disciples. At least twice He had His disciples, most of whom were fishermen, throw their nets over the side of the boat for a catch. Though they had fished unsuccessfully through the previous night, their nets, which were suddenly full of fish, broke under the huge number of fish they caught.

Another time when Jesus' disciples were rowing to the other side of the sea, He fell asleep in the stern from exhaustion. But as He slept, a violent storm arose on the sea and the waves were beginning to sink the boat. When His disciples woke Him, He got up and commanded the winds to be quiet and the waves to be still. Miraculously, the wind and the waves obeyed Him, stopping and growing instantly calm. Jesus was demonstrating His power over the elements He had created.

Another night, Jesus sent His disciples across the sea by boat while He remained to dismiss the crowd and pray. In the middle of the night, while they were rowing against the wind, the disciples saw a figure walking across the water toward them. At first, the disciples thought it was a ghost and they cried out in fear. Jesus called out to them not to worry, that it was Him.

Peter, one of the Twelve, asked for Jesus to permit him to walk to Him on the water and Jesus commanded him to come. Peter stepped down and began walking on the water. Peter lost his courage, began to sink, and cried out for Jesus to save Him. Jesus reached out and took his hand and pulled him back on the water. Jesus entered the boat and immediately the wind and the waves grew calm again.

In all these things, the miracles remind us again of Jesus' power to control creation for our benefit and His promise to restore it and remove death from it forever when He returns on the Last Day.

How much fear do natural events and natural disasters cause for you? How can remembering Jesus' miracles over creation give you confidence?

Jesus Preaches the Kingdom of Heaven

The Lost Sheep

During the roughly four hundred years between the close of the Old Testament and the coming of the Christ, the Jewish people and their religious leaders fell into some bad spiritual habits. In fact, many of them had completely lost their way to God. That is why Jesus said, "I was sent only to the lost sheep of the house of Israel" (Matthew 15:24).

One problem they had was thinking that doing good works and keeping the rules made a person right before God. They carefully controlled the words they said and the actions they did. They tried to impress people with how holy and good they were. But they paid no attention to the evil thoughts and desires in their hearts because they knew no other person could know what was inside their minds. They forgot that God knows and judges all our thoughts and desires. They forgot that our sinful desires show that our works that seem good on the outside are full of selfishness and evil. We can easily fall into that bad habit too.

The Jews also made a habit of judging other people by the circumstances of their lives. If a person was poor, sick, or suffered a handicapping condition, they thought that was clear proof God was punishing that person for his or her sin. When they saw people enjoying good health, riches, or popularity, they were convinced they were good people and God was rewarding their upright living.

This later became one of the biggest reasons Jews refused to believe Jesus could be the promised Messiah. If Jesus was God's Son, they thought there was no way God would have let Him be crucified. So in their minds, the cross was proof Jesus was a lying sinner. It was sad because the whole book of Job in the Old Testament was about this very thing—when bad things happened to Job, his friends thought he was hiding a dark sin. Toward the end of Job, God made it clear to these friends that Job was a believer and was not suffering because of his sins.

Jesus and His forerunner, John the Baptist, were sent to lost sinners to expose their sin. They then proclaimed the Good News that God kept His wonderful promise and sent His Son Jesus to take those sins away. We, too, can put our confidence in the wrong places. Thanks be to God that He is faithful to send a Savior even when we are unfaithful to Him!

Which bad spiritual habit are you most likely to fall for—focusing on impressing other people and forgetting about God knowing your thoughts and desires, or judging God's relationship with yourself and others by circumstances in life?

Jesus' Sermon on the Mount

Jesus' miracles proved He was the promised Messiah. But more important, He taught individuals and crowds about God His Father and how sinners enter the kingdom of heaven by God's grace through faith. In fact, Matthew took three whole chapters in his Gospel (Matthew 5–7) to share a sermon Jesus once preached on a mountain overlooking the Sea of Galilee. It is often called the Sermon on the Mount.

Jesus started with eight sayings that each begin with the word *blessed*. (They are called the Beatitudes, which is the Latin word for *blessed*.) The Beatitudes promise God's forgiveness and blessings when we struggle with how helpless we are to escape our sin. They also promise relief from the mistreatment we suffer from others because of our faith in Jesus, our Savior. Jesus countered the Jewish idea, and the false teaching popular among many Christians today, that God gives success, material blessings, and popularity to those who please Him.

Jesus also explained the right way for us to understand and use the Ten Commandments. The Jews thought the Ten Commandments teach us how we can earn our way to heaven by our good works. But Jesus taught that the Commandments show us our sin and our need for a Savior.

Jesus also taught us how to handle the fears and anxieties we have about our earthly lives. He pointed to the beautiful flowers of the field and well-fed common birds to remind us just as our heavenly Father provides for them, we can trust Him to provide for us. He redirected our focus first to the kingdom of heaven, where we can trust in God to faithfully provide all our other needs.

Think of the goals and dreams you have for your earthly life. *Which of these things could easily take God's place in your heart if you are not careful to remember and study Jesus' teachings?*

Teaching in Parables

Jesus was a fascinating teacher, as we might expect the Son of God to be. Jesus often talked about the kingdom of heaven. But at that time, most of the Jewish people completely misunderstood what the kingdom of God really is (so did the twelve disciples for that matter). They thought it was an earthly kingdom where the Jews would be free, powerful, wealthy, healthy, and strong. And with Jesus healing the sick and raising the dead, they thought their earthly lives would be like fairy tales, perfect and carefree forever.

But life in this sinful world is not like that. In fact, in most fairy tales, the characters go through struggles and difficulties until their happily ever after finally comes, often with prince charming. Life in this sinful world is filled with struggles and difficulties. We suffer from our sins and the sins others commit against us. In Jesus, we have forgiveness and peace, but that does not stop life's difficulties and struggles. We trust in Jesus and know our happily ever after will really only start when our King, Jesus Christ, returns from heaven and makes His creation and each of us believers perfect.

To teach this truth about the kingdom of heaven, Jesus used a special kind of teaching called parables. Parables are heavenly truths wrapped up in earthly stories.

The power of Jesus' parables are the compelling stories and characters He used. His images were fascinating and His stories were so powerful that His hearers remembered them and thought long and hard about them even if they could not at first quite understand what Jesus was really talking about.

One example of a character in a parable is the young man who took his inheritance from his father and wasted it all on wild partying his father would never approve of. He then ran out of money and found himself abandoned, unloved, and starving. In great shame and regret, he came back to his father, begging to be treated like a servant. But surprise! His father ran to embrace him and accepted him back as his son, even killing a fattened calf to hold a great celebration. His older brother stood out in the field, refusing to join the party because he thought his father should have disowned his younger brother instead. The same father went out to urge this older brother to join him in welcoming back his lost brother. Jesus spoke this parable to the proud Jewish leaders who thought it was horrible He was eating and drinking with sinful people who believed in Him.

This painted a picture of God's heart for the lost, as well as how His people should think of sinners God calls to Himself through Christ. Overall, Jesus' parables speak into our daily lives and reveal who God is, what He has done for us, and how we are to see ourselves and others through His eyes.

Make a list of as many of Jesus' parables as you can remember. If you can't remember any, thumb through Luke 14–20. *Which one is your favorite parable and why?*

Jesus Teaches Us to Pray

One day, Jesus' twelve disciples asked Him to teach them how to pray. Many people think God will only listen to carefully spoken flowing prayers. But Jesus taught us to pray to God as if we were little children approaching our father. He even used the Hebrew term *Abba*, which is the word young Jewish children used for father.

When we bring something really important and personal to our parents, they are sometimes shocked, having no idea the things we were thinking, feeling, or experiencing. But when we pray, we never tell God our heavenly Father anything He doesn't already know. He knows everything about us before we ask—He even knows things we can't think to ask. This takes the pressure off of praying and deepens our trust in God.

Jesus also taught us to be confident when we pray, sure that God will answer all the prayers we offer. Our confidence is not because of anything we have done. That is why we don't bargain with God in our prayers by saying "If You will do this for me, I promise to . . ." Our confidence that God will answer our prayers does not come from anything we have done or would promise to do. Instead, our confidence is in everything Jesus Christ did to take away our sins and win a place for us in heaven. That is what it means to pray for Jesus' sake and in Jesus' name.

Jesus promised us that God will always answer our prayers—but that does not mean He will give us everything we ask for like a magic genie. God is our loving heavenly Father. He knows all things and He knows whether the things we ask will help us or hurt us, if they will draw us closer to Him, or if they will drive us away. In His great love and wisdom, He answers our prayers by giving us what we need the most, even if it doesn't feel like it at the time.

Jesus taught His disciples a special prayer, which we call the Lord's Prayer. It starts by lifting our thoughts to heaven where our heavenly Father is seated on His throne, ruling all creation. We ask God to teach us who He is so we know and tell others how good, loving, and gracious He is. We pray for His kingdom to come in our hearts and lives, and that more and more people will believe and grow in faith. We pray that God's will is done, that all people will know Jesus, their Savior, and trust in Him.

In this special prayer, Jesus then brings our attention to this earthly life. We ask our Father to provide all our earthly needs: to forgive our sins for Jesus' sake, give us the power to forgive others from our hearts, and protect us from Satan and every evil.

One of the most beautiful things about the Lord's Prayer is how the Holy Spirit uses it to mold our wills and desires, changing them until we can truly say, like Jesus, "not my will, but Your will be done."

What is something you have prayed for? How did God answer that prayer?

Jesus' Last Supper

Throughout His public ministry, Jesus taught His disciples at the temple, in local synagogues, in towns, in houses, and in wide open spaces.

Jesus taught His twelve disciples a lot the night before His crucifixion, when He ate His Last Supper with them. During that Passover feast, an argument broke out between the Twelve regarding which one of them would be the greatest in Jesus' kingdom. Instead of raising His voice against them for their selfishness, Jesus got up from the table, wrapped a towel around His waist, and began washing their feet one by one the way a servant at the time washed the dirty feet of houseguests. When He finished and sat back down, He taught them that in His kingdom, the greatest will humble themselves to serve others just as He was humbling Himself to serve them.

Then Jesus predicted two really bad sins His close disciples would commit against Him. The first was Judas Iscariot, who would betray Jesus to the Jewish leaders for the small sum of thirty silver pieces. Jesus was careful to make Judas aware that Jesus knew all about it, but He kept the other disciples in the dark, so they kept asking, "Is it I, Lord?" Judas left to go to the high priests, but the disciples thought he was leaving to get something for the meal.

The second was Peter, the one who had seemed the strongest and the most loyal of the Twelve. Jesus predicted that Peter would deny knowing Jesus, and that he would do it three times before a rooster crowed. Jesus pointed out that all of the disciples would flee from Him and go into hiding that very same night. Peter and all of the disciples boldly claimed that would never happen, but Jesus' words proved true.

Jesus then instituted the Lord's Supper to give all of His followers a way to not only remember His suffering and death for their salvation but also to receive His very body and blood for the forgiveness of their sins. In the meal, which God's people take together until Jesus returns, we receive the very body He gave into death as a sacrifice for our sins and His blood He shed as our Passover Lamb. This blood of the new covenant, like the blood of the Passover Lamb, protects us from death and eternal damnation on Judgment Day.

Which of Jesus' teachings from the Last Supper is the most surprising to you?

God's Plan of Salvation Completed

The Garden of Gethsemane

After Jesus finished His Last Supper, He led His disciples out to a spot on the Mount of Olives called the Garden of Gethsemane. There, He left all but three disciples, Peter, James, and John, whom He brought along with Him. Feeling tremendous sorrow, He begged them to keep watch while He prayed, then He went a bit further on and fell on His face in agony.

He pleaded with His Father to take away the cup of suffering set before Him. The bitter cup Jesus was to drink was God's wrath against all human sins—which for us would be suffering in hell forever without end. And He would bear that wrath alone, completely forsaken by God His Father. Jesus begged His Father to take away the cup, to find another way to save humanity—but then He put His Father first by saying, "Not My will, but Yours, be done" (Luke 22:42). That is a great model for our prayers. It is fine to tell God what we would like to happen. But then, like Jesus, we need to humble ourselves, knowing our Father in heaven knows all things and will only do what is best for us, and we need to pray "Thy will be done."

Jesus' struggle did not end in five minutes. The agony, sorrow, and dread came back again and again like waves on the ocean shore. He prayed for about three hours, never giving up until His Father had calmed His mind to accept His will, which was dying on the cross for us.

Jesus teaches us how to pray, especially in those times when praying is hard because we are facing monumental pain, heartache, and terrifying challenges in life. Sometimes praying is hard because we are afraid to let our thoughts and the words of our prayer go to the terrible place they may lead us. This may happen when we pray for God to spare our life or the life of someone we love. Even though it may be easier to distract ourselves with more pleasant thoughts, Jesus teaches us only His Father can prepare and strengthen us for the struggles of life, just as His Father prepared Him for the terrible suffering awaiting Him.

Name one thing that is out of your control and filling you with anxiety or stress right now.

Jesus' Jewish Trials

Jesus had just finished praying and was waking His disciples when a great crowd of soldiers, guards, and priests came into the garden, led by Judas the betrayer. Judas identified Jesus with a kiss, a common greeting. Peter drew out his sword and swung it at one of the mob, cutting off a servant's ear. Jesus commanded Peter to put the sword back in its sheath. Jesus healed the man's ear. The guards grabbed Jesus, bound Him, and led Him back into the city to the high priest's house. Jesus' disciples fled into the night in terror for their own lives.

During Jesus' nighttime trial before the Jewish leaders, He was questioned about many things but kept silent, refusing to defend Himself. The priests brought in false witnesses to testify against Him, but they couldn't even find two witnesses to give the same testimony, a requirement from Moses' law for the death penalty. Finally, the high priest put Jesus under oath, asking if He was God's Son. Jesus answered that He was and they would see Him coming on the clouds of glory on the Last Day. At this, the leaders condemned Him for blasphemy, claiming to be God's Son. They beat Him and led Him off to Pilate, the Roman governor over that area.

While this trial was going on, Peter stood outside with the guards, trying to learn what was happening to Jesus. Servants began asking if he was with Jesus. Three times he was asked and three times Peter denied knowing Jesus or being one of His followers. Just then, a rooster crowed twice, and Peter saw Jesus looking at him and remembered Jesus' prediction at the Last Supper. Peter broke down and wept bitterly. He, like all of humanity, was guilty of denying God and in need of undeserved forgiveness.

What are different ways you or your household deny or hide your faith out in the world? What is one thing you can do to change that and more joyfully embrace your Christian identity in the world?

Before Pontius Pilate

The Jewish priests condemned Jesus to die, then they brought Him before Pilate, the main Roman official for the area. They accused Jesus of three crimes that could be punished by death: causing an insurrection, teaching that taxes should not be paid to the emperor, and claiming to be a king. Pilate did not even investigate the first two charges because he already knew they were false. But he did question Jesus about His kingship.

When Jesus assured Pilate that He was a king but His kingdom was not from this world, Pilate announced that there were no grounds for a charge against Jesus. Pilate should have released Jesus at that point, but he was too afraid of the religious leaders to use this power. So instead he tried some tricks to get the Jewish priests to agree to free Jesus.

Each Passover, Pilate had a custom of giving the crowd the choice between two criminals, one of whom he would release. Usually, these were not dangerous criminals, just political prisoners who had spoken up against Rome. But this time, he took the worst prisoner he had, Barabbas. Barabbas had committed murder in an uprising and was most likely sentenced to die on that middle cross that day. Pilate offered him up alongside Jesus. But Pilate badly underestimated how dangerous the priests thought Jesus was. He was shocked when they convinced the crowds to call for Barabbas to be released and Jesus to be crucified.

Pilate's last gamble was to have Jesus brutally flogged, a violent punishment that often left victims crippled for life. He hoped the Jewish leaders would be satisfied that Jesus suffered enough and was no longer a threat to them. But this did not work either. So to avoid a riot, Pilate consented to their demand and sentenced Jesus to death by crucifixion. Jesus, bombarded by cries of hate, beaten to the point of death, still humbly and willingly went to the cross for the sins of the very people who hated Him and for the whole world.

How do Jesus' words and actions here reflect His heart toward those people— and toward you and me?

Jesus Is Crucified

The Roman soldiers mocked Jesus as King of the Jews. They wove a crown out of thorns and smashed it down on His head. They put a purple robe around His torn shoulders and knelt in mockery before Him, slapping Him and spitting on Him.

As they led Jesus and the other two criminals out to be crucified, Jesus' strength gave out and He fell under the weight of the cross. Since Jesus was too weak and injured to carry it, they forced Simon from Cyrene, a city in northern Africa, to carry it for Him. Finally, when they reached the place of execution, a hill outside the city walls named Golgotha, they crucified Him, that is, they nailed Him to the cross.

During Jesus' first three hours on the cross, from around 9:00 a.m. to noon, sunlight lit up the scene. Rings of people stood around the cross watching Jesus, and those along the road going into Jerusalem mocked Him as a fraud. Priests used Jesus' name to ridicule Him. *Jesus* means "the Lord saves," so they stated, "He saved others; let Him save Himself, if He is the Christ of God, His Chosen One" (Luke 23:35). In response to all this, Jesus prayed, "Father, forgive them, for they know not what they do" (Luke 23:34). This prayer echoes through time to include you and me, and the many sins we commit against God for which Jesus suffered and died.

The two thieves on either side of Jesus also mocked Him for a time. But when one started railing against Jesus again, the other criminal rebuked him. Jesus asked the other criminal if he feared God. The criminal pointed out that they were receiving the just punishment for their deeds, but Jesus had done nothing wrong. Then, believing Jesus was truly the promised King, he asked Jesus to remember him when He came in His kingdom on Judgment Day. But Jesus promised, "Truly, I say to you, today you will be with Me in paradise" (Luke 23:43). The cross shows us both God's wrath for sinful humanity being poured out on Christ and His mercy and forgiveness flowing out to everyone who believes in Him.

Not everyone around the cross was Jesus' enemy. He lifted His eyes and saw His mother, Mary, standing there, and His disciple John. Wanting a believer to care for his mother after He died, He said, "Woman, behold, your son!" and to John, "Behold, your mother!" (John 19:26–27). From that moment on, John provided for Mary.

What is a sin or type of sin you find yourself slipping into over and over again?

43

Jesus' Death

At noon, while Jesus was dying on the cross, the sun stopped shining and darkness fell over the land. Three hours later, at the ninth hour, around 3:00 p.m., Jesus tore the silence with a heart-breaking cry, "My God, My God, why have You forsaken Me?" (Matthew 27:46). Here was hell itself for all to see. He was abandoned and forsaken by God the Father, suffering unbearable agony with no relief, no respite. Hell is not a place of partying as some dream, but lonely isolation and lingering pain. Yet Jesus remained on the cross for us, suffering all that to offer us forgiveness, life, and salvation.

At that ninth hour, Jesus' punishment was complete, and the Father was satisfied that the punishment for all of our sins had been paid in full. The Gospel writer John tells us, "After this, Jesus, knowing that all was now finished, said (to fulfill the Scripture), 'I thirst. . . .' When Jesus had received the sour wine, He said, 'It is finished.'" (John 19:28, 30). Since Jesus completely paid all our debt to God the Father, there is nothing we need to do but believe it by the power of the Holy Spirit. Then Jesus prayed, "Father, into Your hands I commit My spirit!" (Luke 23:46). He gave up His spirit and breathed His last. The prayer to His Father shows Jesus' perfect relationship with His Father had been restored; He was no longer forsaken. The curtain of the temple was miraculously torn in two, indicating that in His death, Jesus had torn down the separation between God and man that started when Adam and Eve first sinned. An earthquake broke open many tombs, and some of the dead in the city miraculously rose to life. This was a preview of the gift Jesus will give to all His people when He returns to raise the dead.

Jesus' body was buried in a tomb by two secret disciples who were members of the Jewish high court. Pilate gave them permission, the tomb was sealed, and a guard was set in front of it in an attempt to prevent any of Jesus' followers from tampering with His body.

> Take some time to ponder Jesus' great gift, suffering the punishment of hell in your place and giving you as a gift eternal life in its place. *What prayer of thanks can you offer for this wonderful gift?*

Jesus Conquers Death

Jesus' Resurrection

As far as Scripture records, there were no human eyewitnesses at the moment of Jesus' resurrection—He was all alone the moment He returned to life. Witnesses only saw the aftereffects of His resurrection. They saw the stone rolled away from the tomb and empty grave cloths lying in the same place they had been when Jesus' body was still within them and His risen body when He appeared to them.

That is what Mary Magdalene, one of Jesus' followers, saw. She immediately ran back to inform the disciples. When Mary Magdalene arrived, she told Peter and John someone had taken Jesus' body. The two disciples ran out to see for themselves. And sure enough, the grave was open and the linen and spices were collapsed down where Jesus' body had been. The two returned home, wondering about what they had seen.

But Mary returned to the tomb and stood there weeping, convinced someone had removed Jesus' body. First, two angels spoke to her. Second, Jesus Himself asked her who she was looking for. She thought He was the gardener. When He spoke her name, "Mary," suddenly the sorrow lifted for Mary, and in wonder, amazement, and recognition, she cried out, "Rabboni!" which means "Teacher." She knew Jesus was risen and alive. She grabbed hold of Him. Jesus told her not to cling to Him, but to go and tell His brothers that He was risen from the dead. So Mary rushed back with the good news, "I have seen the Lord!"

Jesus' resurrection from the dead opens a new day for all of us descendants of Adam and Eve. Satan's trap is broken and death has lost its sting and hold over all humanity. Jesus' resurrection assures us our graves will not be our final resting places. Just as Christ arose from the dead, we, too, will rise to new life with Him in the new heavens and the new earth as He calls us forth from our graves to live with Him in paradise forever.

How does your Baptism connect you to this wonderful story?

Walking to Emmaus

Mary Magdalene wasn't the only one to see Jesus. Other women saw Him and went back and told the disciples they had seen Jesus alive, but the men did not believe them. Later, two followers who were not numbered among Jesus' chosen Twelve travelled out of Jerusalem.

As they were walking along the road to Emmaus, they talked about the whirlwind of things that had happened in Jerusalem, including Jesus' triumphant entry, His popularity among the crowds through the early part of the week, His arrest, His trials, and His crucifixion. And now they talked about the empty tomb and the reports of the women. But these reports gave them no hope or optimism. Before the cross, they had high hopes about Jesus of Nazareth. They thought He would become king and free Israel from the hated Romans. But now their dreams were as dead as they thought Jesus still was.

Then a stranger came up to them on the road and commented about how sad and dejected they looked. They stood there, their faces downcast. He asked what they were talking about, and they were shocked and surprised. How could anyone coming out of Jerusalem not know all the things that had happened there?

The stranger patiently listened as they recalled all that had happened with Jesus, giving them the chance to express their disappointment. After they were finished, He said to them, "O foolish ones, and slow of heart to believe all that the prophets have spoken! Was it not necessary that the Christ should suffer these things and enter into His glory?" (Luke 24:25–26). And then the stranger, Jesus Himself, led them through the Scripture, as we did in the first five of these ten weeks, and "interpreted to them in all the Scriptures the things concerning Himself" (Luke 24:25–27).

The Stranger joined the two men for dinner. He took bread, gave thanks, broke it, and gave it to them, and immediately they recognized it was Jesus. Jesus then miraculously vanished from their company! The two men immediately got up and rushed back into Jerusalem, saying to each other how their hearts burned within them as He talked with them, opening up everything in the Old Testament that had been written about Him. They reached the Upper Room, where most of the Twelve were gathered, and told them how Jesus had revealed Himself to them along the road.

What does the way Jesus interacted with the two men reveal to you about both His mission and His caring attitude toward everyday people?

Thomas

The two men from the Emmaus road burst into the Upper Room, where the disciples and those who were with them were gathered and talking. As they were talking about the stranger who walked with them, Jesus suddenly appeared, right in the middle of them! Frightened, they immediately thought it was a ghost, a logical conclusion since He didn't knock on the locked door or climb through a window. Jesus just materialized out of thin air.

Jesus commanded them to touch Him to see He had flesh and bones, which spirits do not have. He also ate some fish to prove he was not a spirit, for if a mere spirit tried to eat fish, the food would just fall to the floor.

After sharing God's peace with them, Jesus did something amazing. He breathed on them to give them the Holy Spirit, and in this way He gave them the power to forgive sins or withhold forgiveness. Already, just hours after His resurrection, Jesus was forming and establishing His Church, which would continue His forgiving work after He ascended into heaven.

Thomas, one of the Twelve, was absent at this time. When he later rejoined the disciples and heard of what had happened, he refused to believe the testimony of the others who had seen Jesus. He insisted he would not believe unless he saw Jesus for himself, put his fingers in the nail scars in Jesus' hands, and put his hand into the spear mark in Jesus' side. His refusal to believe was not merely because he needed physical proof, but to him, Jesus' resurrection was so preposterous that without God's intervention, he would never believe it.

A week later, Jesus appeared to the disciples again in the same place, but this time Thomas was present. Jesus showed Himself specifically to Thomas, who confessed his faith in Jesus as both Lord and God. Jesus said, "Have you believed because you have seen Me? Blessed are those who have not seen and yet have believed" (John 20:29). We, who hear God's Word and believe today, are truly blessed with the gift of faith!

When are all of us like Thomas?

Fishing in Galilee

After the Passover and Feast of Unleavened Bread were over, the disciples left Jerusalem and went back home to Galilee. Peter decided to go fishing, and a group of disciples went with him. They spent all night fishing but caught nothing. In the morning, they saw a stranger on the shore who asked if they had caught any fish. Hearing they had not, He instructed them to throw their nets on the other side of the boat. When they did, they caught so many fish their nets began breaking. When they pulled the fish into their boats, the two boats both began to sink. The disciple John recognized the stranger and told Peter, "It is the Lord!" Peter jumped overboard and quickly swam in to meet Jesus. The other disciples hauled the boats full of fish to shore.

After their breakfast with Jesus, He asked Peter three times, "Do you love Me?" Each time, Peter assured Him of his love. Jesus was bringing Peter back to his three denials during Jesus' trials. The third time, Jesus asked, "Do you love Me?" Peter was deeply hurt. Jesus then prophesied that in the future, Peter would be faithful to Jesus and show his love by dying on a cross.

Then, on another occasion, Jesus gathered many believers on a mountain in Galilee and gave them the Great Commission to go and make disciples of all nations by baptizing them in the name of the Father, Son, and Holy Spirit, and teaching them to observe all that Jesus had commanded them. Jesus continued preparing and equipping His disciples for their life and mission after He returned to heaven.

What comfort does it give you to think of Jesus as the "stranger on the shore" watching out for you through life?

Jesus' Ascension

Jesus appeared to His disciples in many places and many different ways during the forty days after His resurrection. In the end, these resurrection appearances were so convincing to them that by the Spirit's power, they held firm to their faith even unto death. In fact, every one of the Twelve would eventually go through severe trials and all but one would be martyred, or killed, for their faith.

Jesus met the disciples again in Jerusalem on the fortieth day. He led them out to the Mount of Olives. There, He blessed them, and while He was blessing them, He rose up into the sky and a cloud hid Him from their sight. While they looked up, an angel appeared and told them Jesus would return the same way they saw Him go.

Jesus ascended through the clouds and entered into heaven and took His seat at the right hand of the Father. Like Joseph at the right hand of Pharaoh, and Daniel at the right hand of Darius, Jesus governs all things that happen in creation until the day He will return to judge the living and dead and restore all creation and all of us believers. Though He is at the right hand of God, He is still present with His people, just as He promised. He works through the Means of Grace, the Word and Sacraments that He gives to His Church, to call people to faith, granting them forgiveness, eternal life, and salvation.

Why is it so comforting to know Jesus is sitting on His throne at the right hand of the Father? What does that mean for God's people today?

The End of Our Story

Noah's Flood

Jesus sits at the right hand of the Father in heaven, ruling everything that happens throughout creation. But what is next? When will Jesus return to restore His creation and transform us into perfect, glorious creatures? This week, we focus our attention on the future, when Jesus will return on Judgment Day. What will it look like when Christ returns? The Bible gives us some hints. In this week of reflections, we will first look at the judgment, then the resurrection to eternal life.

The Old Testament describes three events where God judged the world—punishing the ungodly and saving the believers. Today, we begin with the great flood.

Jesus taught that the flood was a real historic event when He spoke about the unbelievers who were swept away in an instant, without any warning but Noah's preaching. Jesus said, "They were eating and drinking and marrying and being given in marriage, until the day when Noah entered the ark, and the flood came and destroyed them all" (Luke 17:27). Consider those words carefully. Jesus made it clear that the devastating flood came out of nowhere and was totally unexpected for everyone but Noah's family. The unbelievers were living life as usual, eating and drinking, marrying and being given in marriage, and suddenly the flood came and it was too late. The flood was worldwide and covered every mountain under the sky with twenty feet of water (Genesis 7:20). Everyone outside the ark died—without exception.

But for Noah and his family, God provided a way to survive the flood. Many years before, He warned Noah of the coming flood and showed him how to build the ark to weather the storm. By the Holy Spirit's power, Noah believed God and obeyed Him, building the gigantic ark that saved himself, his family, and representatives of all the land animals and birds.

Jesus taught us about Judgment Day by comparing the day of the flood to the day of His return: "So will be the coming of the Son of Man" (Matthew 24:37). In other words, people will be going about their lives as usual: eating and drinking, marrying and giving in marriage, planting their fields. Each person will do so with the expectation that life will go on and there will be a tomorrow, but time will run out and it will be too late, as Christ will be here to judge all people. It is a call for each of us to be ready and watching for the day Christ returns. And to share the warning and God's salvation in Jesus Christ with everyone we can.

What does your family do to prepare for potential threats and dangers? What can you do with your household to be watchful for the day of Christ's return?

Sodom and Gomorrah

The second Old Testament judgment we look at in this series was not universal like Noah's flood. It only struck a relatively small region south of Canaan. But it had an eerie similarity to how the New Testament predicts Christ's return.

When Abraham was ninety-nine years old, three strangers came to his tent and he prepared a large dinner for them. It turned out that these strangers were the Lord and two of His angels. The Lord told Abraham his wife would have their son, Isaac, that time next year. Then He sent the angels on and told Abraham they were going to Sodom and Gomorrah because He had heard the cries of oppressed people rising from it. They would see if these cities were filled with violence and oppression. If so, He would destroy them.

Abraham was troubled because his nephew Lot was living as a stranger in Sodom with his wife and two daughters. Abraham bargained with God to spare the place if the angels could find five righteous persons. Not even five could be found, but the angels led Lot and his family out of Sodom by the hand and urged them to flee quickly to the mountains: "Escape there quickly, for I can do nothing till you arrive there" (Genesis 19:22). It was a remarkable show of God's love—His desire to save the righteous actually delayed His judgment on the ungodly. When the fire and brimstone fell upon Sodom and Gomorrah, however, there was no safe hiding place, no way to escape except for the way God provided through His angels for Lot and his family.

What Jesus had said about the time of Noah and the flood, He repeated about this horrific judgment,

> Likewise, just as it was in the days of Lot—they were eating and drinking, buying and selling, planting and building, but on the day when Lot went out from Sodom, fire and sulfur rained from heaven and destroyed them all—so will it be on the day when the Son of Man is revealed. (Luke 17:28–30)

Jesus is clear—the people of Sodom did not expect their lives to end that day. They were eating and drinking, buying with the intent to use that which they bought, selling to use the money from that sale for some purpose, and making plans for the future. But they did not live to see the sun set that day. The same will be true the day Christ returns.

Which distractions (gaming, vacation, sports, personal time) keep you from focusing on receiving God's gifts in worship, which prepare you for the day of Christ's return?

The Destruction of Jerusalem

The third on the list of judgment topics is the destruction of Jerusalem. This event is a bit different than the flood of Noah's day and the destruction of Sodom and Gomorrah in Lot's. We do not have any record of Jesus comparing the past destruction of Jerusalem by the Babylonians to Judgment Day. But He prophesied the future destruction of Jerusalem by the Romans:

> And when He drew near and saw the city, He wept over it, saying, "Would that you, even you, had known on this day the things that make for peace! But now they are hidden from your eyes. For the days will come upon you, when your enemies will set up a barricade around you and surround you and hem you in on every side and tear you down to the ground, you and your children within you. And they will not leave one stone upon another in you, because you did not know the time of your visitation." (Luke 19:41–44)

Jesus picked up on that later when teaching His disciples about Judgment Day:

> And while some were speaking of the temple, how it was adorned with noble stones and offerings, He said, "As for these things that you see, the days will come when there will not be left here one stone upon another that will not be thrown down." (Luke 21:5–6)

Then He warned them to flee the city when they saw the Roman legions marching on the city. Jesus moved on from this destruction of Jerusalem to talk about His coming on Judgment Day. The angel armies will come pouring through the clouds when Jesus returns. Then it will be too late to find relief and rescue in Jesus. Today is the day to sit at His feet, confess your sins, and remember His great sacrifice for you which alone can save you from the wrath to come on sinful humanity when He returns.

What is the most troubling thought you have when you think about Judgment Day? How does the work of Jesus for you on the cross transform how you should view the final judgment of the living and the dead?

The Resurrection of the Dead

The judgment accounts in the Bible remind us of the necessity of repentance and faith in Jesus, which the Holy Spirit gives to us and sustains as we receive God's Word and the Sacraments. But what will the resurrection be like on the Last Day?

We have already looked at Jesus' resurrection. In Baptism, we were connected to Jesus' death and resurrection so we have Christ's own guarantee that we will not remain in our graves but He will faithfully raise us to eternal life. To broaden our understanding and give us greater confidence, we look to other times when Jesus raised dead people to life again.

One instance was a young girl. It was the twelve-year-old daughter of a synagogue ruler named Jairus. When Jairus first approached Jesus, his daughter was dying. He desperately hoped Jesus would get to his house before his daughter died. But along the way, he got word that his daughter had died, and that he shouldn't bother the Teacher anymore. But Jesus immediately told him, "Do not fear, only believe" (Mark 5:36).

When Jesus reached Jairus's home, He found a large number of mourners. He asked what all the commotion was about when she was not dead but asleep. They laughed at Him, thinking they knew better. But Jesus made everyone leave the house except for the child's parents and Peter, James, and John. Then He went into her room, took her by the hand, and said, "Little girl, I say to you, arise" (Mark 5:41). And she arose. Jesus and many books in the New Testament speak of death as a sleep from which Christ will easily awaken us on Judgment Day. Our spirit does not sleep when we die, only our body. Our spirit is immediately brought to be with Jesus when we die. Then when He returns to raise our bodies, He will bring our spirits with Him and return them to our glorified bodies.

A second account came as Jesus and His disciples were walking into a town called Nain. They met another group coming out of town—a funeral procession. Jesus saw the mother of the dead man. He knew she was a widow and that this was her only son, and His heart went out to her. He told her, "Do not weep" (Luke 7:13). He touched the stretcher they were carrying, and said, "Young man, I say to you, arise" (Luke 7:14) and he immediately sat up and started talking. That is the power Jesus has over death. It will be that simple for Him to raise us from our graves with nothing but a word when He returns.

Jesus mourns with those who mourn death but He also talks about death as if it were as light as sleep. How does this give us courage when we think about the day of our death?

53

Lazarus's Resurrection and Ours

We will close our study of Judgment Day with one more account in the Gospels where Jesus raised a dead person. It is extremely fitting to end with this study because Jesus discussed Judgment Day with the sister of the dead man.

Before His own death during Holy Week, Jesus received word that a good friend, Lazarus, was seriously ill. His sisters begged Jesus to rush there to heal him. But when Jesus received word, He remained where He was two extra days. Then Jesus told His disciples to rise, He was going to wake Lazarus up. They thought Lazarus was sleeping and would recover, so Jesus plainly told them that Lazarus was dead and He was going to raise him from the dead.

When Jesus came near, Lazarus's sister Martha came out to meet Him. Jesus told her, "I am the resurrection and the life. Whoever believes in Me, though he die, yet shall he live, and everyone who lives and believes in Me shall never die" (John 11:25–26).

Jesus spoke both about our coming death and our resurrection on Judgment Day when He returns. When we die, only our body dies. Our spirit does not die. But like the repentant thief next to Jesus on the cross, we will be with Him in paradise. Then, on the Last Day when He returns, He will raise our bodies and reunite our spirits with them.

Then Jesus went out to Lazarus' tomb. Lazarus had been buried four days when Jesus arrived. Jesus instructed them to roll the stone away. He prayed to His Father. Then, in a loud voice. He said, "Lazarus, come out" (John 11:43). The man who had died came out, wrapped in linen cloths.

There is nothing magical about the day Christ will return. That is why Jesus said no one will be able to predict it; it will be a surprise to everyone. It will be a common, average, ordinary day just like every day before it. What will make it special is Jesus Christ, the mighty Son of God and Savior of the world. He is the resurrection and the life. He will return with His mighty angel armies, raise all the dead, divide them into believers and unbelievers, and judge them. The unbelievers will be cast out of His creation and confined and tormented in hell forever. The glorified believers will live with Him in the new heavens and the new earth, the creation He will restore when He returns, and we will enjoy paradise with Him forever. That is the story of the Bible, the sweep of the epic salvation story—the story of Jesus and us.

What is the biggest thing you have taken away from reading through and thinking on God's plan of salvation?

MONDAY: Name something bad in your life you wish you could change. *What do you think it would be like if our world and all of us people were still as good as when God first made us?* Wouldn't it be wonderful to live in a world where people were always caring and kind? And if we were the same way too? No one would ever get sick, get hurt, or die. That is the world God made for us and wanted us all to live in. When our sin ruined the world, God sent His Son to save us, and when Jesus returns on Judgment Day, He will make us and His world perfect again. Then all of us who believe in Jesus will live in that perfect world filled with love, good health, and life.

TUESDAY: Try to think of how God wants us to live with our family and friends. *What things can you do at school or home today to make life better for the people God put in your life?* We don't have to wait for Jesus' return to make our world a better place. When we show kindness, patience, and care for our family members and friends, we make their lives a little better. Our friendships grow stronger and our friends will want to know our secret. We can tell them about Jesus' great love for us and the life He gives to us now and when He returns.

WEDNESDAY: *How does Jesus' victory over sin and death change how you live every day? How does it change the way you treat other people?* When other people hurt us, it is easy to get sad, scared, or even mad at them. Jesus understands how it feels to be hurt by other people—people slapped Him, punched Him, and nailed Him to the cross. But Jesus' love was greater than their hate. He died on the cross and rose to life again on the third day. Death was defeated and had no more power over Him or over us. Knowing we will be raised to new life when He returns, we can overcome hate with the love He gives us.

THURSDAY: Think of the last time you got really angry. *What did you want to do? How would it help to think that your anger was like a lion trying to take control of you and God is there to help you take control over it?* By itself, anger is not always sinful. God gets angry when people hurt us—or when we hurt other people. When we get mad, our anger makes us want to do something. Satan and our sinful nature want us to use our anger to hurt other people with our words, or maybe our fists. But God helps us use that power of anger to go and do something good. Maybe we can help someone who is being hurt by others. Maybe we can show love and kindness to the person who is hurting others.

FRIDAY: *How can going to church, reading your Bible, and praying help keep you from wandering away from God like other people do?* When we worship at church and read the Bible, we are remembering how much God loves us and how He gave His only Son, Jesus, to die to save us. His word reminds us that we are sinners who need His love and forgiveness, and the Good News of Jesus makes us sure He has forgiven us and will always take care of us. When we pray, we talk to God. And as we talk to God, He changes our heart to be more like His heart, and He helps us show His love to others.

MONDAY: *How would you feel if you had to leave all your friends and neighbors behind and move to a totally new place?*

Abraham and Sarah were probably pretty scared, but they trusted God. We are sad and sometimes scared when we have to move to new places, but God goes with us and will help us make new friends and be happy in our new home.

TUESDAY: *When in your life does God feel the furthest away or most distant and why? How can Christ's promise that He is with you always offer comfort in those times?*

Your answer may be different from others. If you are sick, or other kids are picking on you at school, or if you are having trouble at home, God may feel very far away. But Jesus, our Savior, promised to be with us always and will give us help and comfort.

WEDNESDAY: *Why do you think there are things that seem more important to us than God's promises in the Bible and our Savior Jesus Christ?*

Our sinful nature makes the things we can see, hear, feel, and hold in this world seem real, while things we can't see seem far away and maybe not real at all. The Bible helps us see God is the only thing that will last and He alone will help us all our life and even when we die.

THURSDAY: Describe a time you were scared about what someone else might do to you. *How did God help you at that time?*

Your answers might include bullies at school or even criminals you encountered or saw on television or in a movie. Remember that God is with us to protect us, and even if He lets other people hurt us, He is there to take care of us.

FRIDAY: *What is one way God has called you to help take care of your family or your friends?* Pray that God would strengthen you to do that with joy and faith.

We can help our parents with chores around the house and being kind and obeying them instead of resisting and making things hard for them. We can help other students at school by watching out for the ones who seem sad and all alone, or are picked on by others, and be friends to them.

MONDAY: Describe something you had to do that seemed way too big and scary for you.
Things that seem too big and scary could include standing up to a bully, giving an oral report, or leaving your friends behind and trying to make new ones after moving to a new home. Each of these scary things can remind us why we need to pray to God and ask for His help.

TUESDAY: *How is the Passover similar to what God did for us in Jesus' suffering and death? How can that change how you look at your friends, family, and classmates?*
In the Passover, the angel of death killed all the firstborn sons in Egypt, including Pharaoh's oldest son. On the cross, God's only Son, Jesus, died. By Jesus' suffering and death, God freed us from Satan's power, forcing him to free us from slavery to sin and death. Because we are free of the fear of God's punishment and hell, we can talk to other people about Jesus, who set them free from being slaves of Satan because of their sins.

WEDNESDAY: Think of the rules your parents, or those who care for you, have for you. *How are they trying to protect you by these rules?* **If you aren't sure, ask them. But be sure to ask them nicely!**
It is easy to think our parents, or those who care for us, make rules because they don't trust us or because they want to take away our fun. But they make these rules to protect us from things that could hurt us, things we can't see or imagine. Examples could be doing our homework before playing, only being on the internet when a grown up is nearby, or going to bed by a certain time on school nights.

THURSDAY: *What is something God commands us not to do that seems like it would be so fun to do? How can remembering Jesus on the cross teach us not to do those things?*
Sometimes we are tempted to break the rules, or to make fun of someone, or to be a bully to someone we don't like. Maybe if we think about how Jesus suffered and died because of our sins, we can decide to do what He did—to love and forgive people who hurt us or make us mad and treat others with love instead of anger or bullying.

FRIDAY: Think of a time when you thought you knew better than God or what God's Word says, and it turned out really bad. Thank God that He remained faithful to you through Jesus, even though you failed.
This might be a time we broke one of our parents' rules or a teacher's rule. Maybe it is experimenting with cigarettes, alcohol, or drugs, or falling into a bad group of people and realizing they aren't as cool as we first thought they were. When we think of Jesus' forgiveness, we know He wants better things for us. He forgives us and give us the strength to change and do what is right and more helpful.

MONDAY: *Why is the relationship of a king to his subjects different than other leaders to the people under their authority? Why, do you think, is it so important for us to think of Jesus as our King?*

The biggest difference between a king and a president is that a king is a supreme ruler. His responsibility is to protect his people from enemies and govern them to protect them from the evil deeds of others. A king's subjects are more dependent upon him than other leaders. Since Jesus is our King, we need to obey Him in everything. But when we remember He loved us so much He died for us, we can be sure His rule is always good, kind, and just.

TUESDAY: *What are some things your friends or kids at school like to do that could be harmful to your faith as a child of God? How can you still be friends without letting those things turn you away from God?*

You may think of drugs or alcohol, or violent video games, or bad videos or movies. Or maybe your friends like to bully other people on social media. For Christians of any age, it is often hard to know how to be a friend to someone who disobeys God. We need to remember that God loves each person on earth and He sent Jesus to die for their sins and ours. We encourage them to stop doing evil and try to show them how much God loves them and wants to protect them from the devil and the sins that would hurt them.

WEDNESDAY: *Who do you know who knows the rules at home or school but keeps breaking them anyway? Why is it important for us to do what God wants and obey our parents and teachers?*

We all know a brother or sister, a neighbor, or a classmate who knows the rules but breaks them anyway. That is how the Israelites acted. They knew they should serve God, but they loved their sins too much. It is important to serve God by obeying our parents and teachers because God wants to protect us from the terrible things those sins would do to us, especially if they would destroy our faith and lead us away from Jesus forever.

THURSDAY: **Describe the darkest time in your life when you felt things would never get better.** *What did God do for you?*

Maybe there was a time you had to move from your friends to a new, strange place. Maybe you had to be in the hospital. Even in these times, when it seems like things will never get better, God watches over you, teaching you to trust Him and making things work together for your good. God will keep His promises and help you through all the bad times to come.

FRIDAY: *Who has God put in your life to take care of you and help you grow into a man or a woman?*

Certainly parents, aunts and uncles, grandparents, and teachers come to mind, but it could also be your coach, teacher, pastor, someone from church, or many other people.

MONDAY: Consider a position or role you have at home, at school, or on a team. *What opportunities has God given you to love and serve your neighbor?*
These neighbors include your parents, grandparents, teachers, and coaches. God has placed them in authority over you. They also include brothers and sisters, friends, neighbors, classmates, and teammates you can protect, encourage, and treat well. You should share God's love with them for Jesus' sake.

TUESDAY: *Who are the people who govern your city, state, and country? Why should we pray for them?*
You may have heard some things from your parents or those who care for you. But whether you agree or disagree with the people who govern our land, remember that God has put them there so we should pray for Him to give them wisdom and genuine concern for all the people God has placed in their care. Also, they are sinners who need God's forgiveness as much as we do, and Jesus is the only King who is perfect and loved us enough to die in our place on the cross.

WEDNESDAY: *What does it mean to live each day as God's redeemed child in Christ while also living your life with other people that God loves?*
Being God's children washed in Jesus' blood, we can have hope and peace no matter how difficult our lives get. Living with other people and remembering God loves them as He loves us helps us befriend them and give them encouragement when they are troubled or afraid.

THURSDAY: *What difference does it make to know that Jesus experienced the same kind of childhood you are experiencing?*
Often it feels like no one knows what we are going through, how difficult and unfair life can be. But whenever we know someone who has gone through the things we go through, we know they understand us. It is so much better that this person is Jesus, the mighty Son of God who not only understands us but also has the power to do things to help us.

FRIDAY: Think of a time when God's Word called you to repent and change one of your habits or an attitude. *What impact did that have on your life as God's redeemed child in Christ?*
Habits or attitudes could include lying, being short-tempered, being jealous, or being mean to others. When God's Law exposes our sins, His Gospel brings us to our Savior and empowers us to change our life to please God as we live in friendship with those around us.

MONDAY: *What does Jesus' experience of being tempted in the wilderness teach you about facing temptations to sin?*

Jesus did not use His divine wisdom or power to resist Satan. He used the same tools that we can use—the words of God in the Bible. This is why it is important to read and learn our Bibles so Jesus can help us see through Satan's lies and deception and make wise decisions that please God.

TUESDAY: Consider the main roles you have at home and at school. *What opportunities do those roles give you to tell others what Jesus has done for you through your words and actions?*

You may feel limited because of your youth or because you must obey parents and teachers. But being humble and obedient will make you stand out, and it might give you the opportunity to explain why you don't resist and rebel like other young people do.

WEDNESDAY: *How would your life be different today if you and your family did not have to worry about sickness, injury, or death?*

You may have experienced sickness personally or in the life of a friend or family member. If you have not, perhaps you can think of a grandparent who died before you ever knew them. Even though you don't miss them in your lives, stop and realize that despite never knowing them, you had a grandparent who would have loved you dearly.

THURSDAY: *What is one blessing God has given you in your life that you easily overlook?*

It is so easy for us to take God's gifts for granted. If you are having a problem thinking of anything, think about someone you know who has a struggle in their life. The fact that you don't have that struggle shows how God has blessed you and you are probably taking it for granted. Other blessings can include family, lack of war, crime, poverty, and so on. Even if you are facing struggles now, you can always be thankful your problems aren't worse than they are.

FRIDAY: *How much fear do natural events and natural disasters cause for you? How can remembering Jesus' miracles over creation give you confidence?*

Are you extremely afraid of violent storms or tornado warnings? Remember that those storms still know Jesus' voice the same as when they obeyed Him during His life on earth.

MONDAY: *Which bad spiritual habit are you most likely to fall for—focusing on impressing other people and forgetting about God knowing your thoughts and desires, or judging God's relationship with yourself and others by circumstances in life?*

When we only try to impress other people, we can be puffed up by pride and falsely think God is happy with us. That is why Jesus teaches us to open our hearts, minds, and souls to God, asking Him to clean away all the sin. On the other hand, when we try to judge how God feels about us or about other people by the things happening in life, Satan will often use that to drive us away from God. When times are good, we may drift away from worship, Communion, and studying God's Word because our success is telling us God is fine with us. And when we go through times of failure, sickness, or suffering, he tries to convince us God is punishing us. That is a lie because God already punished Jesus for us.

TUESDAY: **Think of the goals and dreams you have for your earthly life.** *Which of these things could easily take God's place in your heart if you are not careful to remember and study Jesus' teachings?*

There is nothing wrong with having dreams and goals for your life. When we love God first and use those dreams and goals to help others and show them God's love, they are a blessing. But if we think achieving those goals and dreams will bring meaning, happiness, and joy to our lives and we forget God, they will be a curse instead. That is why sometimes when we pray and ask God for something, He chooses not to give it to us. He wants to bless us, not drive us away.

WEDNESDAY: **Make a list of as many of Jesus' parables as you can remember. If you can't remember any, thumb through Luke 14–20.** *Which one is your favorite and why?*

Jesus' parables have a way of teaching something about God, or maybe what it is to be a believer in a sinful world. Sometimes a parable speaks directly to a situation happening in your life. Some of Jesus' parables are difficult to understand. For those, it is best to pray for God to teach you and to give you patience until you can understand them. Sometimes our understanding of a parable grows after we go through things in our lives that we have not yet experienced.

THURSDAY: *What is something you have prayed for? How did God answer that prayer?*

Sometimes when we don't get what we asked for, we are tempted to think God did not answer our prayers. But when we ask in faith for Jesus' sake, there is no such thing as an unanswered prayer. Sometimes God gives us what we ask because He knows it is the best thing for us. When He chooses not to give us what we ask, He may be saying no because He wants to give us something better than what we are asking for. Or He may intend to give us what we ask, but only when He knows the time is right.

FRIDAY: *Which of Jesus' teachings from the Last Supper is the most surprising to you?*

Jesus washing His disciples' feet confronts our self-centeredness and our reluctance to help other people around us. His prediction of Judas's betrayal, Peter's denial, and His other disciples abandoning Him reminds us not to rely on our own strength, but to recognize our weakness and run to Jesus for forgiveness and confidence. Holy Communion makes the sacrifice of Jesus' body and blood on the cross personal as we receive them in the bread and wine.

MONDAY: Name one thing that is out of your control and filling you with anxiety or stress right now.

Pray that God would strengthen your faith and trust in Him during this time. Learn from Jesus to not give up praying when it gets hard, emotional, and when you feel like you are drowning in your stress and fear. Be sure to remember how Jesus prayed and how He completed His suffering and death for this lost and broken humanity.

TUESDAY: *What are different ways you or your household deny or hide your faith out in the world? What is one thing you can do to change that and more joyfully embrace your Christian identity in the world?*

Sometimes we try to blend in with other people by using swear words, telling obscene jokes, or joining in with bullies—especially bullying other Christians who are being ridiculed for standing up for their faith. Here are a few things you can do to embrace your Christian identity: watch your language, don't participate in events you know are wrong, or stand up for someone who is being bullied.

WEDNESDAY: *How do Jesus' words and actions here reflect His heart toward those people—and toward you and me?*

Jesus' prayer, "Father, forgive them, for they know not what they do," shows that Jesus' love for His fallen human creatures is greater than the pain and heartache we inflict on Him. He understands our sinful nature, how we are often unaware of the sins we commit and don't really realize how powerful God's wrath is. Yet Jesus was willing to endure that wrath to save us all.

THURSDAY: *What is a sin or type of sin you find yourself slipping into over and over again?*

Take some serious time today to think about your sins and your need for forgiveness, asking God to forgive your many sins for Jesus' sake. Ask God's help to do better, then go about your day rejoicing in the forgiveness that Jesus won for you, forgiveness that can't be taken away.

FRIDAY: Take some time to ponder Jesus' great gift, suffering the punishment of hell in your place and giving you as a gift eternal life in its place. *What prayer of thanks can you offer for this wonderful gift?*

You can write your own prayer or think of a hymn, psalm, or Bible verse where someone prays to God for forgiveness and thanks Him for that forgiveness (see Psalm 32; 51; 116; 118).

MONDAY: *How does your Baptism connect you to this wonderful story?*
In Baptism, Jesus connected you with His death and resurrection. So you died to sin and your sin died to you. Even though your body will eventually die if Jesus does not return first, just as Jesus rose from the dead in glory, when He returns He will raise you to new and glorious life.

TUESDAY: *What does the way Jesus interacted with the two men reveal to you about both His mission and His caring attitude toward everyday people?*
First, Jesus noticed their sorrow. Second, He listened quietly as they poured out their feelings, disappointments, and anxieties. When they were done, He took them through the prophecies in the Old Testament Scriptures, which had foretold His suffering, death, and resurrection. And He explained why all of that was necessary for our salvation. It reminds us we are free to pour out our hurt, anxiety, and our complaints to Jesus, and He is ready through His Word and Sacraments to comfort us and fill us with hope, peace, and joy.

WEDNESDAY: *When are all of us like Thomas?*
Thomas usually gets a bad reputation as a "doubter," but we all experience doubts about our faith. In fact, none of us would have saving faith without the Holy Spirit working through the Means of Grace. Say a prayer, thanking God for the gift of faith, which we would never have without the Holy Spirit.

THURSDAY: *What comfort does it give you to think of Jesus as the "stranger on the shore" watching out for you through life?*
Jesus knows everything we are going through—especially our fears and frustrations. He is always with us and will always protect us, provide for our needs, and save us from sin and all our enemies.

FRIDAY: *Why is it so comforting to know Jesus is sitting on His throne at the right hand of the Father? What does that mean for God's people today?*
This position means that Jesus is in control of each and every thing that happens throughout His whole creation. He limits and controls evildoers, He protects and provides for His Holy Church and all of us, His brothers and sisters, and He leads us to our eternal home.

MONDAY: *What does your family do to prepare for potential threats and dangers? What can you do with your household to be watchful for the day of Christ's return?*
Wise families make plans and preparations for what to do in case of a fire, tornado, or earthquake. They run tests from time to time to make sure they are ready. We can watch for the day of Jesus' return by thinking of that day each time we pray "Come, Lord Jesus." We watch for it when we pray the Lord's prayer ("Thy kingdom come") and say the Apostles' or Nicene Creeds and reach the end where we confess our belief in "the resurrection of the dead and the life of the world to come." Finally, whenever we learn of someone's death—especially a sudden, unexpected death—we can remember our earthly lives will end one day, so we need to repent of our sins and trust in Jesus so we will always be ready.

TUESDAY: *Which distractions (gaming, vacation, sports, personal time) keep you from focusing on receiving God's gifts in worship; which prepare you for the day of Christ's return?*
Some distractions keep us from going to church altogether; others occupy our minds when we are at church and keep us from truly being made ready for Judgment Day by confession and receiving God's forgiveness through the Word and the Sacrament of Holy Communion. Ask God to remind you earthly things are temporary and will all one day pass away, and to set your minds on Jesus' return and the wonderful, joyous life that will be ours forever when He returns.

WEDNESDAY: *What is the most troubling thought you get when you think about Judgment Day? How does the work of Jesus for you on the cross transform how you should view the final judgment of the living and the dead?*
For some Christians, it is the concern that we won't be ready when that day comes. Our greatest danger as Christians is giving up on worship and Bible reading so we are not ready when Christ returns. For many Christians, it is not so much concern for ourselves, but for our family members, friends, neighbors, and co-workers who do not know Jesus. The certainty of Judgment Day should fill us with concern for them so that we pray for them and find opportunities God gives us to share Christ's salvation with them.

THURSDAY: Jesus mourns with those who mourn death but He also talks about death as if it were as light as sleep. *How does this give us courage when we think about the day of our death?*
Thinking of our death can be frightening, because at that time, there will be nothing anyone on earth can do to help us—not our parents, brothers and sisters, friends, doctors, anybody. But Jesus gives us comfort because He has already experienced death on the cross where He won forgiveness for all our sins. He defeated death for us when He rose from the dead. He describes our death like falling asleep so we learn to trust Him and know that He will conquer our death and raise us to new, eternal life when He returns.

FRIDAY: *What is the biggest thing you have taken away from reading through and thinking on God's plan of salvation?*
You may think it was seeing all the different ways the Old Testament revealed different aspects of Jesus' suffering and death on the cross and His resurrection and how He would save us from our sins. Or maybe you see Jesus' life and ministry in a new way. Perhaps you have a new understanding of Jesus' death and His resurrection. Or maybe you have a keener attention to the end of this world when Jesus will return unexpectedly to judge the living and the risen dead and bring believers into life eternal.